INDIA INCORPORATED
THE MISSING LINK

INDIA INCORPORATED
The Missing Link

By

K.S. Ramachandran

ANMOL PUBLICATIONS PVT. LTD.

NEW DELHI - 110 002 (INDIA)

ANMOL PUBLICATIONS PVT. LTD.
4374/4B, Ansari Road, Daryaganj
New Delhi - 110 002
Ph.: 23261597, 23278000
Visit us at: www.anmolpublications.com

India Incorporated: The Missing Link

First Published, 2003

ISBN 81-261-1425-8

PRINTED IN INDIA

Published by J.L. Kumar for Anmol Publications Pvt. Ltd., New Delhi - 110 002 and Printed at Mehra Offset Press, Delhi.

CONTENTS

PREFACE

When I thought of asking various experts to join a debate on major issues of management under a liberal environment, at the back of my mind was the worry over how Indian corporates and non-corporates would be able to cope with the competitive regime that had emerged with the removal of quantitative restrictions on imports on April 1, 2001. Though initially it did not occur to me that I should pay some attention to the prospect of India beginning to function as a global village, as I read through the papers that I got from Dr. M.B. Athreya, Dr. Neelamegham, Dr. D.H. Pai Panandiker, Mr. V. Raghuraman, Mr. V. Suresh and Mr. Y.K. Gupta, I realised the urgency of the task.

Part I of the book has virtually written itself, with the known and acknowledged fears of competition from abroad and also the opportunities thrown up by the discarding of quantitative curbs globally dictating the manner of visualising India as a global village. This was an enjoyable exercise and I sincerely hope that this offering would set the ball rolling on developments beyond the limited response to the immediate post - April 1, 2001 scenario. After all, more than dialectics, what should matter to the graduation of the Indian economy to the ranks of the most competitive members of the international community is its fighting spirit. This, obviously, is not in my hands.

As of today, India Inc. is characterised by what I call the missing link, but the goal of this particular endeavour is to set right this infirmity. This phenomenon became glaring as I proceeded and it was but inevitable that this should become the caption of the book. Addressing the malady cannot be the Government's job and must become a high priority of the players themselves. Now, what is this gloomy aspect of the management of the Indian economy? In one word, it is a total want of urgency about the fast developing future. There are no doubt titans riding on individual dynamism, but there are pygmies galore ever ready to settle for less and doing precisely that. Governance is engaging the attention of several people, but I am not quite convinced that the right aspects are addressed. Global corporate frauds have promptly provoked a thrust on transparency and improved regulation, but the gains of liberalisation could be maximised only with efforts towards promotion of healthy governance focussing on responsible management without loss of a competitive spirit. Accountability among managers must be fostered and what is worrying is that those in Government having a hand in policy formulation are retreating into the regulatory mechanism of the past. This retreat is exemplified by a proposal mooted in the Companies (Amendment) bill, 2003 that seeks to reduce stakeholders to a minority in the board of directors and giving majority representation to independent outsiders. The concept that the perceived independence of directors without a stake is synonymous with acccountability is not only difficult to accept but could also aggravat the want of urgency, that I mentioned earlier, in the management of the Indian economy.

Mr. Krishna Murari Sinha has provided exemplary secretarial support, while Mrs. Y. Vijayasri has lent the requisite research and editorial backing.

—K.S. Ramachandran

Part—I
INDIA: A GLOBAL VILLAGE

1

MANAGEMENT: REALITIES Vs ILLUSIONS

Ideally, managements should address realities, but often managers in the hot seat assume illusions to be realities and seek remedies to these where the perceived circumstances pose problems or try to use these as a distinct advantage where the perception is that gains are imminent. Managers suffer as a consequence. But, while one manager should, for purposes of self-protection, learn from another's mistakes, this does not always happen. Managers do not compare notes, for there are no friends in the world of competitive management and there are only rivals or, worse still, those who will come handy and can be exploited. The old saying is that there is something like honour among thieves, but if you watch closely you will find this either conspicuously absent or only superficially present among managers.

I am not suggesting that the two are comparable in terms of their professional demands. Yes, I must concede that managers have to do – and often do – a lot of things that those in the other glaringly dishonourable profession would envy. But, obviously, no book on management can get away with the outrageous comment that managers do no more – or less – than thieving. This book cannot take such a risk. Even so, as to questions of honour, while I am not competent to say anything on what all thieves do or don't for their professional success and advancement, I can declare myself on managers without fear of contradiction or embarrassment. There cannot be too much honour among managers given the compulsions of day-to-day management. One manager's honour is another's dishonour and *vice versa*. Though quite unfamiliar with the ways of thieves, I can hardly believe that there can be any honour among them knowing the demands of their profession.

THE ELEVENTH COMMANDMENT

Those who have opted for robbing and burgling as a profession are also managers, though without all the gloss that goes with the latter, and those of the tribe who are not professional enough to avoid the extreme risks that go with their jobs land up in jail. Those whom we call managers and to whom this book is addressed are no less in danger of losing their high profile positions and their credibility as managers if they fail to pursue a consistently professional course. While they are required to be very clever, yet if they indulge too often in sharp practices and are not too careful they could also find themselves behind bars. The eleventh commandment on corruption, justifiably, is not to get caught and this the managers and thieves alike have to respect.

Managers in the corporate and non-corporate sectors are paid to capitalise on the weaknesses of their rivals and the loopholes in laws, rules and regulations. But, in all this they have to be on the right side of the statute book. While they have to save on taxes, this necessarily has to be done through planning leading to avoidance and not through blatant evasion. Rival organisations have to be weakened and even swallowed up, but only through measures that do not breach the law. The prolonged battle that Microsoft is caught in warns against managements being too greedy and clever. At a lesser level, several managers in different parts of the globe are put in the dock for offences as varied as insider trading, stock price rigging, manipulation of accounts, dumping etc. In one sense, those who get caught are treated no better than thieves, their careers ruined because they tried to do too much for themselves.

Clearly, managers have to be successful without getting into a collision course with the regulators and the courts. In the last two years or so, a number of globally reputed corporates have been ruined, and wantonly, by their CEOs and their advisors. Now, they are in the dock in the United States and elsewhere.

Those in the two professions can and do get deceived by illusions. This deception is partly behind all the trouble that they get into. Illusions have to be distrusted if the idea is to succeed. Such distrust should be natural and spontaneous. Illusions make the situation far too bright to be true. Such brightness should by itself be dissuading to people with sense. For, behind danger there is always too much light. A businessman who seems much too rich must be doing a lot of hanky panky. The corporate that is really doing well will tend not to show off. There are, no doubt, corporate czars the world over with flamboyant lifestyles, with private jets thrown in along with various other perks. But, there are also CEOs like Mr. Bill Gates, who use their earnings to promote social justice cutting across national boundaries.

STIGMA AND RESPONSIBILITY

The difference between the two professions is that there is a social stigma attached to one, while the other carries with it a lot of social respectability. It is true that criminals are into politics in a big way. The underworld has its hands in business activity as well and the parallel economy which sustains legitimate industrial as well as commercial activity on a significant scale has a strong nexus with the underworld. It goes without saying that neither the political leaders nor the captains of industry and business would ever want to demonstrate their links with the criminal forces. The growing stress on managerial professionalism, however, is leading to a lot of transparency in industrial and business management. Yes, the Government's revenue department is getting no respite from evasion of sales tax and understatement of production leading to reduced payment of excise duty. The more the State Finance Ministers seek to add to revenue through a widening of the sales tax base and enhancement of tariffs, the more the businessmen try to reduce their tax liabilities. But, with greater globalisation and Indian companies listing their scrips in NASDAQ, accounting practices necessarily have to become cleaner. No wonder, CEOs are looking exclusively for legitimate sources of finance and also cushion – borrowings from FIs and credit from banks, capital raised from the market within as well as abroad and the rebates and subsidies from the Government. Reforms have forced the Indian industrial and business fraternity into commercial and financial practices that are more and more consistent with globally accepted standards. As a consequence, what all would have passed muster in the past are getting dumped into the dustbin of history. Yet, in the wake of all the mega scandals that have hit the corporate world in recent years a lot of caution would be warranted in respect of certain ugly practices designed to inflate stock value.

PRESSURE OF COMPETITION

Nevertheless, competition is making it incumbent on managements to become more and more clever and to adopt measures in several spheres that would give their constituents an edge over their rivals. While any step that is even suggestive of fraudulence rules itself out, CEOs and their teams increasingly have to enhance competitiveness allround. This means that nothing is taboo as long as the rules are not violated. The present thrust on governance, significantly, does not overstress on avoidance of corruption and such other matters that concern the nation's vigilance machinery. The watchword is accountability. While the advocates of responsible governance do not make light of issues like bribery and influencing policymakers and those executing policies and administrative decisions through dubious means, still the message sent out is that promotion of professionalism and accountability will itself take care of the worries loudly voiced by the Central Vigilance Commissioner.

The governance aspect of competitive management acquires considerable importance in the light of the strains and stresses of increasing globalisation. The withdrawal of quantitative restrictions on imports effective April 2001 had posed a challenge even to the best performing corporates and non-corporates in the country's industrial and business arena, what to speak of those which had been surviving only because of the protected market syndrome. The challenge has become tougher with further opening up in the exim policy for 2002-03 and 2003-04. In this context, governance is effectively an agenda for thwarting the efforts of overseas producers to snuff out the locals. With dumping by Chinese and other manufacturers assuming threatening – if not ominous – proportions, domestic companies have got to fight harder to survive.

Those in the export arena may themselves have to adopt measures that are close to dumping, which though cannot risk being classified as such. After all, they cannot but pursue what their rivals resort to. In fact, they have to do the same thing better and in ways that the WTO would accept. Some of WTO's rulings in recent months virtually set the format for global business strategies. We know only too well how the Asian Tigers have consistently outwitted the U.S. manufacturers to capture a massive market in the latter's own domain. The South East Asian economic crisis has not blunted their global competitiveness. There are, thus, lessons in the recovery of the regional economies in recent years for Indian companies and the SSIs with export as a major line of their activities. But, care has to be taken to ensure that we are always on the right side of WTO. We should not ever fall foul of it.

NO EXERCISE IN DIALECTICS

Knowing that innovativeness is the real key to phenomenal success, CEOs and those assisting them will have to develop strategies and action plans that render dynamism and fighting spirit the core of operations. When we say this, we involuntarily, and spontaneously, argue for an approach that virtually says yes to any act that is designed to outsmart all others in the fray. Ethics and morals, however, have to be respected, if not for anything but certainly to send the message across to all those segments of the community which matter that the company in question is trustworthy. Social accountability is no exercise in dialectics but an aspect of competitive performance globally. When merchandise comes from outside without any quantitative restrictions, the Indian market truly becomes a global village. No goods produced within are assured of an easy market and selling is really going to be a tough proposition as the flow of cheaper and better quality goods from overseas accelerates.

The transformation of the domestic market into a global village need not be a catastrophe, but could easily become one if the level of Indian industrial and business preparedness fails to rise to the demands of globalisation. Yes, the policymaker and executor have a role in such preparedness insofaras dumping in any form can be effectively prevented and no more than a level playing ground is assured for whosoever enters the Indian trading arena. But, the real effort has to come from those in the fray. Indian manufacturers have to acquire the fighting spirit as much as the competence needed in the present circumstances. Excuses will not do and the need of the hour is excellence.

Economists are required to be guided exclusively by economic rationale, but often they let themselves be influenced unduly by subjective assessments. Facts are twisted as a matter of course to arrive at value judgements that are pre-determined. This may seem a somewhat harsh and arbitrary verdict, but the trouble with this profession is that hard facts are not always allowed to dictate. Those in Government are led by the latter's declared priorities and in industry and business by the wider goals of governing interests. Data and policy inputs are played up or down depending upon what the Government's goals are and this is the story of industry and business also. In the past, clearances from Government were sought and given on the basis of twisted facts as part of collusive arrangements between the licensing authority and the concerned corporate. With liberalisation and delicensing, such collusion should have become minimal, but it is doubtful if greater entrepreneurial freedom for investment decisions in terms of both new investment and expansion of existing capacity has dispensed with the kind of perceived compulsions leading to manipulation of critical data.

SPEAKING THE MASTER'S VOICE

Just as there is no great independence for the economists in Government service, their counterparts in industry and business generally have to speak the master's voice and go along with those who lead. The Government has its own bureaucracy so has the corporate. In either case, the hierarchy dictates. Economists whether they are in Government or industry are not the policy makers. They are also not the enforcing authority. Their job is to provide the data that would facilitate sound policy formulation. While the Government economists know that they are paid to vindicate the policies and actions of the leadership – and go along with a Prime Minister who wants an impossible growth rate in GDP – the role of their counterparts elsewhere cannot be any different. The latter also have to bow to the demands of those in command.

Thus, there is as much scope in industry and business as in Government for frustration among meritorious economists who would like to assert themselves. But, this does not dissuade members of the profession from leaving the academic community in favour of advisory positions elsewhere. Indian universities and research as well as management institutes cannot boast of keeping the drain of the more competent economists in check. Rather, the truth is that the best in the discipline opt for positions in World Bank, IMF, UN organisations, prestigious research bodies and academic institutions abroad if they do not like the lack of independence in Government and industry and business. What much of the academia – I mean that part which carries a reputation – prefers to do is to keep one foot firmly in positions that keep proclaiming its intellectual credentials and be on the look out for jobs that pay. Lien is a convenient arrangement for academics with ambitions. That their contribution to the parent bodies is getting more and more negligible does not seem to bother anyone.

The consequence is an overall decline in the quality of intellectual activity, which is inevitable given the fact that work responsibilities in both the parental institutions and elsewhere are getting only a cursory treatment. Research is indifferently carried out, facilities for serious research and academic activity are misused and half-baked books and papers get churned out with gains for none but the professors and researchers who are the architects of such diversions. These gains are strictly monetary, which is quite natural considering the general lack of application and commitment. Most universities have nothing worthwhile to declare by way of their intellectual output, with their more reputed members staking their reputation to get profitable contracts elsewhere. Their extra-curricular achievements help to enhance their professional reputation and they readily assume that they are moving closer towards the Nobel Prize.

CHANGING COLOURS

Till some years ago, few members of the economic academia would have anything to do with the media and lobbying and organisations like industrial associations and chambers of commerce. Now, economists have no qualms about openly serving newspapers and being lobbyists. In the past, most economists would not want to be seen as anything but leftists. Even in the aftermath of liberalisation, some of those who belonged to the discipline had serious doubts about the merits of reform and they did not hesitate to come out with their concerns.

But, there are hardly anyone with a leftist ideology. It is not that reform has changed attitudes and perceptions. Well before India declared itself to be committed to reform and opening up, university professors and research consultants were falling into the trap set by international institutions. No wonder, those who were getting lucrative deals (in rupee terms, with a steadily eroding rupee) from the World Bank and IMF had no reservations about the declared views of the two bodies in the forefront of liberalisation, and what all went with it. Studies espousing the cause of free trade and a fully convertible rupee raised no protests in seminars. Curiously, the economists who voiced concern about the reform impact on poverty alleviation were those with fat pensions from the Brettonhood twins. The staff papers of World Bank and IMF have consistently expressed views that were contrary to the known policy postures of the multilateral watchdogs. But, it was acknowledged that these papers were not the policy documents of the two institutions, and such expression of 'academic' independence as these demonstrated, obviously, was quite irrelevant to the progress of the discipline.

The 'princely' pensioners of the Brettonwood twins did not run the risk of their pensions being cut off. They were also free to give up their earlier concerns about the neglect of the poor under a deepening process of reform and liberalisation in return for prestigious – if not influential – jobs in the reformist regime. You may call it intellectual dishonesty if you like, but one supposes, that all this is consistent with the spirit of free enterprise that liberalisation preaches.

2

WHO WANTS ECONOMISTS?

Strangely enough, while in the regulatory years there were times when the Government and private industry alike had sought to show that the latter could play a meaningful part in developmental planning – beyond its customary lobbying function – under reform, corporate strategists have not been accommodated in either the Planning Commission or the Government departments. It was by way of an exception to the general rule that an acknowledged expert in power planning and management was made the Union Power Secretary. But, this was done at the conclusion of a decade of reform, which really is not saying much about professionalisation. Yet, this would have been the most logical course to adopt to give planning an increasing business orientation. Knowing that the five year plans and the annual plans of the Centre and various State Governments continue to have a considerable impact on the development process because of the massive investment involved, such an orientation would have been warranted since mid-1991 when we went on the reform path.

Corporate economists are nowhere in the formulation of reform strategies and in mid-way corrections. Unlike members of the academia, they cannot even appear on television and write newspaper articles. They have to remain quite as faceless as the *sarkari* economists. Managers with functions such as HRD, finance, marketing, industrial relations, materials management, inventory control, production management etc. have avenues to express their views – without coming into conflict with the perceptions of CEOs – but the public is in the dark about the role of economists in industrial planning and management. Is it that big industry and business have no need for economists?

Can it be that in the perception of industrial houses economists serve no purpose beyond ghost writing for CEOs and senior managers? The apex bodies of industry and chambers of commerce employ economists at various levels, but the latter are used mainly to make lobbying work better. The top corporates have constituted research outfits, but the intention, ostensibly, is to send the message across to the community at large that they can do other things than merely making money. The publicised provision for research is part of the image building exercise. This is no joking matter. That in this era of business-led reform industrial houses have no place for economists is a signal that virtually mocks at a discipline, which is trusted globally to prepare strategies for development and decide the fate of entire nation states.

FOR LECTURE HALLS, NOT MARKET PLACE

Captains of industry cannot be unaware that when the World Development Report of the World Bank in the mid-eighties came up with a well argued strategy for market-friendly development across national barriers, that could only have been the handiwork of economists with credentials good enough to appeal to the World Bank. Top CEOs lined up to hear the only Indian economist to have won the Nobel Prize, Prof. Amartya Sen. But, how many economists are there in the top brass of corporate empires? Financial institutions and banks do employ economists in their task of project evaluation and determination of the viability of investments, but the latter are required to interact with corporate finance managers primarily. Obviously, in the perception of corporate leaders, economists only have a macro function and cannot be trusted with micro responsibilities. In that sense, economists are treated on par with the management gurus – both are meant for lecture halls and seminar rooms – and the true market place cannot function with the help of theorists and can only be sustained by men and women competent to handle specific functions. Effectively, economists cannot be good managers – this is the business perception.

What impact such wanton neglect of economists is having on the quality of management it is hard to say since people with a strong economic background have not found their way into senior managerial positions. In this context, it must be said that with the growing induction of young people, who have done courses in business management or administration, corporate bodies did not feel the need for managers with an understanding of economic theory as well as applied economics. This is not offered as a suggestion, but as a possible – even justifiable – explanation for the absence of economists in corporates at policy making levels. Obviously, the thrust on economics that is relevant to managers in formal management education has obviated the involvement of members of the academic and research academia in corporate decision making at the micro level.

But, this reasoning does not still answer the wider issue whether micro economics is not really consequential to business management. For one thing, the economics that is taught as part of the curriculum of management institutions has only a narrow focus. For another, the attitude and perception of students of MBA courses are those of would–be managers, who generally are brainwashed into believing that they have to be practical and down to earth and should not let themselves be fooled by theories and concepts. Intellect is generally kept out of the formal study programmes arranged for those preparing for a career in management. In sticking to this straitjacket, teachers and students alike gloss over the fact that the best known managers relied largely on their unique intellect to achieve phenomenal success. The record of men like Iaccaca and Welch only underlines the supremacy of intellect over other factors. True leadership is essentially a mental process and instinct that has triggered the most remarkable successes in the management arena globally reflected a strong ideology. Thus, no great harm would come to the market place if the hard task of management was entrusted to men and women with excellent academic credentials.

NOT ON THE STRENGTH OF NUMBERS

Ultimately, managerial excellence is achieved not on the strength of numbers alone. Power docs matter, but the emergence of corporate giants over a period world-wide only symbolises the uniqueness of the will power of certain visionaries. Mr. Bill Gates may be seen as a villain by the anti-trust diehards in the United States, but the dominance of Microsoft – and the *Financial Times* verdict that it was the best performing corporate in the world in 1999 – spoke loudly of the intellectual acumen of its founder. In India, there have been similar success stories underscoring the phenomenal power of the intellect. When the ex–Vice President of the United States could take up teaching of journalism and successive U.S. presidents have taken corporate leaders in their cabinets, there is no reason why the academia should not be involved in management, not in a peripheral but in a fullfledged capacity.

A core aspect of management is strategy formulation and this goes on almost all the time. Strategies are evolved and corrections made as and when necessary. No corporate or any other organisation, big or small, can do without strategic responses. The manner and style in which these responses are worked may vary from unit to unit. A shop keeper, who is the sole proprietor, will handle this all by himself. He may talk things over with a friend or his wife and decide what to do. A corporate body will hold not one but several meetings and might take recourse to outside help by way of consultants. In recent years, McKinsey and Company is all over the place, with banks, public sector industrial undertakings and private sector companies seeking out the internationally reputed consultancy firm for support but, regardless of whosoever is involved in the task what really delivers the goods is intellect. Consultancy organisations do use economists besides other specialists in working out packages for their clients.

ECONOMICS IS IN PLAY

Economics is in play wherever decisions are made, even where there are no specialists. Petty shopkeepers do use economic principles without realising it, and without all the airs that highly reputed economists put on. Economists have a tendency to make everything look very complicated and this could be one reason why CEOs are not very comfortable with those belonging to the discipline. Models are allright for text books, but in regard to management strategies do need to be spelt out in terms of achievable performance and the hurdles to cross rather than confusing econometric exercises. Economists have to speak the manager's language and their inability or reluctance to do this is an obvious explanation why managements are happier without economists who cannot mend their ways.

Now, the question arises if good management needs high sounding names and reputations or principles that work. We all know that the best results are achieved with sharp managerial reflexes. Such reflexes certainly would have a strong economic base. There can be no doubt about that, but we should all remember that behind some of the most phenomenal corporate successes have been some non-conformist decisions by the CEOs. The basic economic rules were broken. For instance, the question has never been satisfactorily answered whether a situation of strong or emerging recession could be met effectively with corporates and small businesses alike falling in line or alternatively by doing something dramatic – like outrageously assuming that recession was not pervasive enough to cause worry. Traders do not have to accept that sales were slack and stop showcasing goods. Such non-conformism could weaken the recessionary forces in the economy if this is demonstrated by a large number of sales outlets. I can never forget an important principle of good management being explained perhaps unwittingly and quite casually in one of the soap operas *Dynasty* : Showing off a comfort level that did not exist to create the impression that all was well. The head of the dynasty has problems managing his empire, but keeps his millionaire status intact by presenting an expensive diamond necklace to his wife. The latter is uncomfortable with the gift. It is in this context the principle comes out clearly through the big man's daughter accustomed for long to an affluent life – that in times of trouble the best course is to show that the czar has millions of dollars to play with and to squander away.

RESPONSIBILITY AND ACCOUNTABILITY

Intellect, however, serves little purpose without responsibility and accountability. In the case of a petty shopkeeper, he or she bears the full consequences of the decisions taken. This gives the decision-maker a high sense of responsibility for whatever happens. It is hard to say if success comes automatically to people with this quality. But, it would be quite foolish to argue against responsible behaviour. In fact, accountability must be accepted as an important aspect of sound management regardless of whatever organisation is involved. This part of managerial conduct should not be dependent on remuneration alone and no manager can compromise on this because of financial considerations. The commitment that is deemed natural in small proprietor concerns and is associated rightly with a total stake in the future of the firm must become part of everyone who serves an organisation.

Obviously, a workman cannot assume that his responsibility ceases with his/her specified duties. Likewise, a supervisory official should not think that nothing more need be done beyond fulfillment of the orders received to the satisfaction of the immediate boss. The manager should not also be satisfied with being on the right side of the CEO. While loyalty is a must, this should essentially be to the job, not to the superior official. It is wrong for the management to promote yesmanship to the point where job takes the second seat to respect for heirarchy. Dissent should never be for dissent's sake but, if there is little scope for participative management then motivation gets effectively discouraged. The management style should be such that everyone feels involved in whatever is done and is planned to be done. .

In justified and responsible dissent intellect is more reflected than in indiscriminate yesmanship. One can even say that intellect gets banished in a management culture where orders are given only to be carried out without any questions asked. There has to be wider consultation and a serious effort must be made to go beyond the rules of hierarchy. Suggestions must be sought and the principles of delegation should be loosened to promote participatory involvement. Everyone down the ladder must be encouraged to speak out, if needed, against organisational policies. The divide that has got embedded in management has to go and unions and the top brass must sit together to evolve ways of fostering independence at different rungs of the management structure.

TAXING THE GREY CELLS

The grey cells within everyone in an organisation must be taxed. Globally, the good conduct certificate by McKinsey and Company does count a great deal. One must grant this, but the expensive contracts to internationally reputed consultancy organisations do not have to come as a hurdle to efforts to tickle the brains of workers, supervisors and managers in every organisation. After all, expertise is not the exclusive preserve of extravagantly paid experts. The grey cells of lesser mortals can also provide the same expertise at a lesser cost if encouraged to give off their best. Motivation is known to get good results and can be relied upon to provide the same kind of suggestions and action plans to bring about significant improvements in overall performance. Ultimately, what matters is the quality of leadership, which is largely an intellectual activity. This does not demand much formal education. As for individual brilliance, the example of two brothers in Kerala some time ago achieving so much proficiency in the sphere of information technology as to receive recognition from one of the computer majors in the United States underscored the supremacy of raw intellect over formal education. The fact that the programmes developed by the two young men had earlier failed to impress the big computer outfits within the country only reflected the rigid mindset of managements even in the supposedly fastest moving segment of the Indian economy, which also boasts of paying the greatest regard to human excellence.

Obviously, Indian corporate leaders do have to sharpen their intellectual levels so that they can look beyond pre-determined notions to pick true talent. As of now, the big industrial houses refuse to look beyond the prestigious management institutes to recruit would-be managers. As for engineering, the choice is limited to the outgo from the IITs. Ironically, the 'gems' of the latter are increasingly opting for the IAS. In respect of staff selections for computer and software engineers, again, the cut-off point is the output from institutions carrying the reputation tag. Campus visits have a narrow focus and HRD managers refuse to learn from their mistakes where either the selected management or other trainees quit to take up other positions or those who stick fail to deliver. With a proliferation of management, engineering and computer institutes, it is not easy for the HRD departments to be indiscriminate in staff selection. Discrimination is thrust on them by the fact that more and more young people are available year after year for recruitment. The fear among recruiting teams is quite natural that they should avoid taking those who might not get the nod from their superiors. CEOs know that they are not paid to promote talent outside. Their priority is to tap qualified professionals who can fit into their groove. When they confine their choice to candidates boasting of the best formal education, they believe that chances of failure are minimised.

BEYOND FORMAL EDUCATION

Academia and *gurus* are free to think otherwise. I presume, a book such as this has to recognise the compulsions of CEOs and their supporting managers. I cannot set an agenda on staff selection and training to managements that they cannot realistically fulfill. There has to be a balance between ideals and management limitations. Yes, I am convinced that formal education is not the true passport to managerial excellence, and raw talent should not be neglected merely because it lacks a formal endorsement by way of a prestigious degree or diploma. But, I cannot gloss over the difficulty of managements in finding talent outside the reputed coaching institutions. Nevertheless, some attention has to be paid to the neglect, that is rampant, of brilliance that has not got formalised. Perhaps, to start with, at least the best run corporates must begin scouting for genius in homes, in slums and in villages. True genius should not be allowed to wither away. Intellect must be fostered both through formal education and other avenues. Along with campus visits, industrial houses must organise regular trips to the urban slums and villages and use community centres in cities and the village panchayats to catch talent before it is too late. Obviously, the managers entrusted with this delicate task should be capable of drawing out the best from the people whom they meet.

In a protected market, anything goes and this has been the basis of management in the pre-reform industrial economy. No doubt, values have been changing since the start of reform but not fast enough to prepare most, if not all, manufacturers for the massive invasion of consumer goods in particular, with the withdrawal of quantitative restrictions from April 1, 2001 and subsequent liberalisation of industrial and trade policy. The 2002 and 2003 exim policies have opened the doors wider and the Government has declared its resolve to deepen the reform process further. While there are certain safeguards open under the WTO regime, these only add up to buying time. Ultimately, the local outfits either must stand up to overseas pressure or be prepared to exit. Some of the Indian manufacturers have begun sourcing their input needs from the very suppliers in China and parts of South East Asia, which have given the finished goods manufacturers of this region the cost competitive edge that really mattered in international markets. But, effectively this is no more than expediency.

NO BARRIERS, NO NATIONAL LOYALTIES

Logically, in a liberal trading environment there are really no barriers, no national loyalties. In a federal structure, diverse states do take care of sub-national commercial interests through preferential levies for local manufacturers, and in India the Centre and the apex court have repeatedly decried the State Governments' flagrant of manipulation of sales taxes to favour entrepreneurs within. Some fiscal protection can, with justification, be offered to Indian manufacturers against the might of their competitors from the South East Asian and pacific region. But, essentially, whosoever wants to survive and flourish has to fight. Nothing else will work. The Indian response to the emerging situation from the side of the Government and the affected Indian manufacturers has been somewhat mechanical. We do not have to deliberate on the policy and administrative courses open to the Government. The anti-dumping measures, where dumping is established, and protective levies can work only to a limited extent. From the side of manufacturers, cost competitive sourcing of inputs from abroad will help the final goods manufacturers but will spell ruin to the suppliers of the very same inputs within the country. But, this option is not open to everyone and, obviously, several small and tiny producers operating in diverse product areas with the backing of reservations on the one hand and duty exemptions on the other are going to be rendered totally helpless. Their workers are certain to lose their jobs. But then, one must consider the fact that SSIs have been exporting in a big way. No doubt, tax rebates have helped, along with the other safeguards provided. Even so, the units which have become established exporters can be expected to fight things out when overseas goods flow in. This flow began even before quantitative restrictions were formally withdrawn. If the impact has been really severe, several SSIs should have pulled the shutters and a considerable workforce should have been thrown out of their jobs. There is no evidence yet that this has happened. Yes, it would be wrong to assume too much from this. Complacency is not the right agenda for success in a daunting business environment. But, a Cassandra-like response is not also warranted. Since we proclaimed our commitment to liberalisation, there has been a lot of exposure of managers to internationally reputed *gurus* and, as we noted earlier, it has also become fashionable for the big Indian corporates to seek advice from transnational consultancy organisations on matters of management structure as well as policy. All this exposure would seem wasted if our manufacturers can do no more than source their input needs from China and South East Asian countries.

3

FACING UP TO GLOBALISATION CHALLENGES

In standard responses to an emerging challenge, intellect is less at work than it would be with dynamic strategies. Such dynamism, however, does not come easily to a leadership that is accustomed only to taking advantage of a protected market and is quite unfamiliar with the uncompromising demands of a competitive market. It is now more than a decade since the Narasimha Rao Government adopted a reform format for the Indian economy. This is a sufficiently long period for the competitive spirit to grow, but we all know that even the spurt in imports of low cost consumer goods in recent months and withdrawal of quantitative restrictions of overseas goods have failed to provoke the kind of tactics that have in the past several years pushed the Asian tigers to the forefront of global trade deceleration. While the same tactics have made a swift recovery possible from the crisis of 1996, Indian manufacturers have not come out with an approach that would facilitate a combative spirit developing in the long preparatory phase ahead of the shiffer challenges of globalisation.

NO CAUSE FOR PANIC

Even now, despite the growing presence of Chinese goods in the Indian market there is really no cause for panic. When the threat first emerged, the former Indian Industry and Commerce Minister, Mr. Murasoli Maran, though not quite dismissive on the impact of the influx of Chinese merchandise, had made it clear that panic was not going to be the Government's policy reaction to removal of quantitative curbs on goods from abroad. This was a positive stance, even knowing that in the WTO straitjacket scope for policy and administrative deterrents to free flow of diverse commodities and products, especially from low cost suppliers like China and the Asian tigers, was limited. But, representative bodies of industry then had not taken a similar stance. Rather, they put pressure on the Government to stagger the import flow.

This was no different from the pressure tactics of Indian industry and business in the long regulatory years. Attitudes have not changed since then, not withstanding the dynamism of certain corporates. The question is whether this has a lot to do with the quality of business leadership or whatever goes in its name. Intellect is a key issue and under the old controls and regulations — which could be loosened or tightened selectively depending on the favours given or taken – this was there no doubt, but used largely to influence policymakers and administrators at different levels and in different positions. In the changed environment of considerable de-regulation, intellect must be made to deliver in regard to giving Indian industry a strong combative edge not only abroad but also on its own turf, that too with the minimum of fiscal and other props. This is a big test and our task would be easier now with the quantitative curbs on imports fully gone, if only our management techniques have a strong intellectual base and, not only that, these are designed to fight and win rather than to defend and survive.

POORLY THOUGHT OUT

Any strategy that relies on imported inputs to ward off the East and South East Asian onslaught, obviously, is poorly thought out. Even granting that manufacturers should concentrate exclusively on the fulfillment of their own interests and should be insensitive to what happens to those within the country from whom they have long been sourcing their inputs, the intellectually sound approach would be to keep their loyalty to their local input suppliers intact and devise a futuristic strategy that advances the interests of input suppliers and final goods manufacturers simultaneously. This is no exercise in gimmickry, but makes good strategic sense in the long run. Loyalty between suppliers of inputs and final producers is no academic issue, but should be the main plank of any long-term strategy for competitive production and marketing.

In his memoirs, the former member of the Syndicate (of the undivided Congress before the late Mrs. Indira Gandhi used the populist plank of economic radicalism to strike her own path), the late Mr. D. P. Mishra recalled an observation on Mrs. Gandhi by a journalist: "Ideology was her weapon, she wasn't a weapon of her ideology." That comment had been provoked by the populist ways of the former Prime Minister. Mrs. Gandhi's populism is among the subjects discussed in my work *Economics of Politics and Politics of Economics: A Business Perspective* (2002). If we look at the achievements of charismatic corporate leaders of the past and present, who simply overwhelmed their contemporaries with their genius, can we say anything different? In retrospect, notwithstanding the Emergency that blotted the record of Indian democracy, Mrs. Gandhi was no different from the egoistic and ruthless corporate Czars who gave their business czardoms the glitter that was simply matchless. Ideology or populism is not only a political instrument. This is also part of the corporate armoury, though this bears a more acceptable description such as strategy or game plan.

CORPORATE POPULISM

Long ago when Mr. JRD Tata flew a plane and followed it up with a regular schedule of air flights he was being either populist or ideological or both. Anyone who looks beyond his/ her time and is daring to be non-conformist can be bracketed with Mrs. Indira Gandhi. Her son, Mr. Rajiv Gandhi would have attracted the comment quoted by Mr. Mishra if only he had, instead of the unlikely Mr. P. V. Narasimha Rao some years later, translated his initial urge to put the Indian economy on the liberalisation path. The result of his retreat at the New Delhi AICC session in the face of protests from the socialist diehards in the Congress party was that Mr. Rao did everything in the realm of economic policy making to merit the same description of Mrs. Gandhi. As a politician, Mr. Narasimha Rao could be written off by posterity as nothing short of a disaster. But, as the architect of reform, he will always be remembered for daring to turn his back on the Nehruvian gospel of socialism and a dominant public sector.

Any successful CEO can be easily compared with Mrs. Gandhi for other reasons, more so her dictatorial ways. Mr. Mishra's memoirs throw a lot of light on the politics of deception in the period prior to the first split of the Congress triggered by Mrs. Gandhi's urge to marginalise the Syndicate representing the old guard in the party. But then, which corporate empire is free of similar deception? Mr. Mishra himself was known as the latter day Chanakya and those who know enough of the goings on in Indian business empires would also be familiar with the corporate version of Machiavelli. Behind the rise and behind the fall of several companies can be seen the calculating hand of managers whom Mr. Mishra and Mrs. Gandhi alike might have envied.

No battles are won or lost in the market place without stratagems and conspiracies. Intellect is a key part of these stratagems and conspiracies, whether these help win a battle or contribute to a rout. After all, Chanakya and Machiavelli relied essentially on their grey cells to work out winning strategies. In the decades leading to reform, their versions in Indian businesses were mainly concerned about manipulating the regulatory wheel to their advantage and against their perceived rivals. The licensing mechanism duly attracted such a manipulation. Under reform, one would expect the Chanakyan endeavours to be directed against rival corporates, though obviously less and less through the Government and its agents and more and more through market mechanisms, the stock market, marketing network and the consumers.

NO GIMMICKRY FOR CORPORATES

But, there is a substantial difference between the proclaimed ideology in political populism and what is implicit in business endeavours to capture the customers' hearts. The politician is looking at gains that are not monetary in explicit terms although knowing the ways of political parties we cannot rule out a narrow financial motive in the populist acts of Governments. There are wider goals, especially capture of power. The Election Commission has, no doubt, come out with the code of poll conduct, which restrains parties in power from taking recourse to flagrant measures of securing electoral gains. But, since the code comes into force only after the issue of poll notifications, this gives a lot of scope for exercise of poll-dictated populism. The same freedom is not open to corporate CEOs. The latter will want to sell cheap and indulge in gimmickry to sway the buyers. But, no gimmickry can work if the product or service offered fails in terms of quality.

Not only that, in a competitive environment, no one manufacturer or service provider can use these tactics without the rivals doing the same thing even better. Today's ad campaigns are marked by almost everyone in the market place offering free sales. "Buy two, take one home free" is the popular—or should I say populist? — Slogan. I do not know which ad agency started this ludicrous game. But, the message that gets across is that the manufacturer has inflated the price so much that there is no obvious loss in offering something extra *gratis*. Is this what should be the response to the emerging pressures in the market place? Politicians can get away with anything, but this rules itself out to market players. The 2001-02 Railway Budget was the most flagrant exercise on poll-dictated largesse in recent years. The standing committee for railways as well as the Khanna panel had been provoked by a critical financial situation to demand tough measures of revenue mobilisation. Yet, the minister in charge let the compulsions of the assembly poll in West Bengal take precedence over grave financial constraints. The minister virtually flaunted a bottom less bucket when the strains on the nation's real network cried loudly for an over flowing bucket, and with a strong bottom. Such a thing even the most whimsical CEO cannot dare visualise.

NO ROOM FOR SHORTSIGHTEDNESS

Manufacturers and service providers can ill afford to be shortsighted. It would not do for them to catch the attention of new buyers only to lose it in a short while. This caution is warranted even where the market has something different to offer. I recall the bitter experience of *Financial Express* in 1995 when the *Economic Times* suffered a prolonged strike. The decision was taken to bring down the price of a newspaper whose circulation was very small compared to that of the *Economic Times* and, given its very limited popularity, the *Financial Express* needed to keep its cost economics right by pegging the price at cost plus. It was not surprising, therefore, that price parity with the *Economic Times* created a financial crisis which remained unresolved for quite a while. I am able to recall this strategic error because I was then a Senior Editor in the *Financial Express* and had serious doubts about the decision taken. This matched the reckless populism of the 2001-2002 Railway Budget, which preferred not to tax the rail user even in the face of grave compulsions.

The *Financial Express* was not a bad — unsaleable — product in the print media before it was sought to be given what was pompously described as a new look during 1994-95. Till the early eighties, it did not lag too much behind the market—business and economic print media — leader, the *Economic Times*. Significantly, this offering by the *Indian Express* group made up for its limited circulation through substantial earnings from advertisements. Don't ask me why and how the *Financial Express* was able to secure advertisements far more than warranted by its circulation. But, it was a fact. Yet, this aspect was no justification for a policy not to grow up. When all financial newspapers went pink (only in colour, not otherwise), the idea was to underline their comparability to the globally circulated *Financial Times.* Going pink, however, had to wait until the nineties. Prior to that had, however, come the shift of focus from economic reporting, analysis and commentaries mainly to a dominant coverage of business-related developments.

The *Economic Times* stole a march over the *Financial Express* from the late seventies through its thrust on research and its better marketing. Its editors demonstrated a dynamism that the *Financial Express* was not able to muster. By the mid-eighties, the *Economic Times* began to assume gigantic proportions. The *Financial Express* did strive during 1988-89 to put up a bold front through a sharp business orientation. But, obviously, that proved too late. The launching of a new look *Financial Express* during 1994-95 also failed to make an impact. There are several important lessons in the spectacular rise of the *Economic Times* as much as in the fall of the *Financial Express* for managers outside the print media also.

During the period when the *Economic Times* had a strike, a critical factor emerged. This was not so much in the sphere of product development as in marketing and in promoting customer loyalty. The *Financial Express* showed a singular lack of urgency in marketing the new look *Financial Express* as a viable substitute for the *Economic Times.* Marketing executives of the *Economic Times* were there in full strength at the distribution centres in the early hours on every day of the strike to check the gains to the *Financial Express.* While the leadership of the *Financial Express* failed to support the price parity with the *Economic Times* with sound marketing, the market leader fought hard to prevent loss of buyers. It kept a close watch on areas which took *Financial Express* instead. It was that spirit which contributed to the fact that once the strike ended the net loss was minimal.

LESSONS FROM THE MEDIA

Subsequently, the *Financial Express* enhanced its price,

which came as a belated acknowledgement of the market reality that it was no more than an also ran against the awesome might of the *Economic Times*. You may call the situation prevailing in the business print media one akin to what the Microsoft is enjoying at the expense of the other constituents of the infotech sector in the United States. The only difference is that the *Economic Times* is doing nothing that Microsoft is blamed for. There is no exploitation and what is happening is characteristic of a condition of monopoly — the leader capitalising on its might and leaving the others to crawl while it was itself sprinting. A consumer product that bears a comparison with the *Economic Times* is the Colgate toothpaste which towers over all other brands. A common factor is the power — quite legitimately used — of the leader. In neither case has power deteriorated into exploitation. The circumstances allegedly surrounding Microsoft in the U.S. infotech market, yet, are not irrelevant to the Indian context.

For a product or service to make a favourable impact and also keep this intact, the strategy has to be multi-pronged. Primarily, what is offered must appeal to the buyer and, what is more, this appeal must remain notwithstanding severe competition. This is easier than done since with competing forces in a free market there is always a better alternative. The customer always has more than one option and his/her loyalty is constantly tested. There is never anything like a lasting influence. Worldwide, there have been instances of parvenus worsting the leaders and reaching the top, through a combination of grit on their part and lethargy on the part of products which lost the battle. This has happened in controlled and protected economies. In India, well before the onset of reforms, new competitors had emerged in diverse segments of industry to dislodge supposedly well entrenched market leaders. The rise of Reliance and Essar over a short period of time reflected the power of entrepreneurial dynamism.

Today's winners have to encounter challenges that are different from those of yesterday pioneers. But, obviously neither had an easy run. Tatas and Birlas, no doubt, had before them a virgin territory and they faced little or no serious competition in the product areas they chose to enter. But, Nehruvian socialism saw to it that they could not venture into the core sector and they had to accept the dominance of public sector in segments that really mattered. Yes, the industrial licencing policy and procedure and those provisions of the MRTP act bearing on growth of concentration of economic power outside the public sector did not hinder private sector development as much as the statute threatened to do. But, clearance of new investment proposals severely tested the patience of interested industries, and not all could stand up to the bureaucratic drill. With reform, there is greater entrepreneurial freedom, but the market is tougher with several people in the fray. The FERA, 1973 nearly ruled out the entry of MNCs and the situation now is dramatically different. There is more transparency in business deals and the manipulation that was part of the permit-quota raj has given way to openness. The consequence is that investors do not have the kind of cushion that their counterparts earlier had enjoyed.

POST-REFORM ENVIRONMENT

And once the product is out there is no certainty that it will automatically win wide acceptance. Well before a product gets ready for the commercial launch, everything has to be done in terms of market development. This, again, is tougher with reform. The protected market earlier generally gave the product an easy turf. While there were some product failures, most manufacturers got through easily. Entrepreneurs knew that they did not have too much of a problem promoting their products and services since competition was limited and also weak. With far too many sellers, the post-reform business environment demands greater wooing of consumers. Superior quality must be matched by competitive price as well as service. Obviously, the market can no longer be taken for granted. If the ad campaigns presently focus increasingly on freebies, that is largely because of mounting pressure on manufacturers and service providers. The uncertainty associated with the truly free market is what we are now witnessing. This is set to grow with the removal of quantitative restrictions on imports and with the flooding of the Indian market with various goods spread over diverse segments of industry.

As for the Government, it is having to heed WTO's diktat precisely at a time when the economy is still caught in a slow down and has to recover, and very fast. Returning to early, 2001, the response of the Union Budget for 2001-02 had not just been pragmatic but dynamic. It more than made up for the electoral populism of the Railway Budget. The Union Finance Minister had, in accepting the responsibility for preparing the manufacturing sector in particular for the post April 1, 2001 scenario, signalled to Indian industry and business that they should honour their side of the bargain. I have been arguing consistently that reform is essentially the task of the respective players themselves. My research studies for the Institute of Management Technology, *Managerial Challenges of Reform* and *Corporate Preparedness for Competition* had focussed on that aspect. While the Government must continue to come up with stimulants to growth, or recovery as the circumstances warrant, measuring up to the pressures of removal of quantitative curbs on imports and a further deepening of the process of trade-related liberalisation demands the fullest attention of industry and business.

In fact, the budgetary initiatives in the sphere of customs duties, while offering significant protection to domestic suppliers, were designed to make them fight things out. This emerged easily from the 2001-02 projection of a revenue gain of Rs. 4,677 crores annually from the proposals made in the budget as against a loss of Rs. 2,128 crore in respect of customs duties. The strategy, obviously, was that protection would be provided only against imports and manufacturers would not get any support by way of excise relief to boost demand. One must recall that such relief was used earlier by Mr. P. Chidambaram as Finance Minister to stimulate recovery, which however, did not come about. Mr. Chidambaram's complaint then was that the various manufacturers had let him down by not passing on the intended price incentive to consumers. His successor saved himself some embarrassment by not using excise duties exclusively to reverse the slow down in the economy.

STIMULATING RURAL DEMAND

In all fairness to the NDA Government, the 2001-2002 Union Budget proposals went beyond the narrow back-up to the abolition of all quantitative limits on imports. Significantly, an answer to the demand-induced recession was sought in the rural segment by way of a serious impetus to farm production with an enhanced Rs. 64,000 crore credit flow to agriculture. The nation had to wait for a decade for a formal launch of the exit agenda and this was provided in the Budget. Industrial units employing less than 1,000 workers could down shutters without prior permission from the Government. The Industrial Disputes Act was sought to be amended during the budget session itself. Earlier, I referred to the issue of reservation of a number of product areas for the small scale sector. This I did in regard to the repercussions of the removal of quantitative restrictions on imports. The Finance Minister should have taken a bold step towards de-reservation of products all this long earmarked to the small-scale sector, but he only proposed removal of 14 items from the SSI list. This was a drop in the ocean. Also, there was some doubt whether the Government could really get the Industrial Disputes Act amended, given the reservations voiced by the constituents of the ruling coalition on efforts to deepen the process of reform. On privatisation also, despite a favourable ruling by the Supreme Court on the proposed disinvestment of Central Government equity in BALCO, it seemed unsure if the Government would be able to push disinvestment really hard. There was no doubt a flurry of activity, but the controversy over VSNL's actions under the changed management following divestment, for a time, kept everyone very busy. After this was sorted out, other hurdles emerged and sale of Government equity in oil PSUs still remains a non-starter.

Apart from the Union Budget and fiscal initiatives outside this annual exercise, there are always interventions — corrective or stimulating — in the shape of interest rate adjustment. For quite some years now, the Reserve Bank of India has consistently followed up the budget presentation in Parliament by changes in interest rates. In 2001 also, the nation's central bank opted for such changes with the bank rate being brought down to seven per cent. Managements have looked to RBI for support in respect of bank credit. With the economy badly needing a kick start and the Finance Minister choosing to give a boost to demand in the rural economy, the RBI rightly sought to reduce the cost of bank credit further. A year later, we saw a further relaxation in terms of a lower cash reserve ratio, a step intended to render credit freer. The credit policy for the slack season of 2003-04 announced by the Reserve Bank Governor in April, 2003 pushed the bank rate and the cash reserve ratio to a further low. Managers should find in the move an added stimulus to raising output. Allowing for the inventory build up of finished goods as well as inputs to take care of the rising demand in the initial period— this itself may not take place immediately - production in diverse segments of industry should start rising only after a while. Psychology does always play a part in either a deceleration or recovery, and depending on how strong it is the pick up can come sooner rather than later.

The Finance Minister voiced an expectation of industrial production overall rising by 7-8 per cent during fiscal year 2001-2002, but given the extent of deceleration witnessed during 2000-2002, this was by no means substantial. A dynamic industrial sector should have achieved much more than a modest recovery forecast in the 2001-02 Union Budget and that for 2002-03 as well as 2003-04. In presenting the Union Budget for 2003-04 even though the compulsions of globalisation did not quite take the backseat the Finance Minister necessarily had to contend with the slow recovery of the economy, the aggravating fiscal pressure and the constraints of impending assembly elections over and above the eight per cent growth set for the tenth plan. I have referred mainly to the 2001-02

Union Budget because of its bearing on the repercussions of the April, 2001 removal of quantitative curbs on imports. The support so thoughtfully provided for capital formation and the protection offered to a number of industries against cheap imports by way of selective hikes in import duties added up to a industry-friendly approach. The cut in the bank rate facilitating a reduction in the bank lending rate should enable managements to make the most of this approach. Globally, the interest rate cut should have helped our export-oriented manufacturers and producers take advantage of the earlier recovery of the U. S. economy triggered by the cut in the rate of interest by the U.S. federal reserve. Also, if the U.S. recovery helps absorb the competitive products of China and the Asian tigers, the pressure on the Indian market from these suppliers can get reduced. This will come as some relief in the face of the predictable flooding of the Indian market by cheaper overseas products. However, corporate frauds in the United States have come as a set-back to growth of the U.S. economy.

THE FIGHTING SPIRIT

Effectively, the ball is in the court of domestic industry and business, and it is for the latter to give a fight to low cost suppliers from abroad. India is certainly being forced to become a global village, but much how Indian it will remain in the coming years will depend not so much on how supportive the Government is as on the fighting spirit of the various players. This spirit must show itself strongly to the point where business leaders should be able to tell policy makers not to bother any more with their problems but to leave them free to resolve these as best as they could. Such an assertive dynamism should be on display, not by fits and starts, but as a lasting aspect of business policy and operations. All this long, this has not been the case, with the political leadership and bureaucracy repeatedly being persuaded to provide the platform for competitive performance of indigenous manufacturers. This lack of initiative and perhaps, even courage, must go, sooner rather than later.

The optimism generated by the Union Budgets for 2001-2002 and for 2002-03, however, did not mean that this major instrument of fiscal activism was really going to push the economy on to the dynamic path. Indeed, Mr. Yashwant Sinha's handiwork went the way of the dream budget of Mr. P. Chidambaram earlier and Mr. Sinha duly paid the price by getting shifted to the Ministry of External Affairs. Mr. Jaswant Singh, who switched portfolios with Mr. Sinha showed greater sensitivity towards the investor and middle class than his predecessor, but his approach to growth and matters of liberalisation and reform, duly reflected in the 2003-04 Union Budget, was no different. Specifically, on growth, if agriculture fails to turn from a laggard of the fast few years to a driving force — despite the enhanced provision for this sector and the increase in bank and institutional credit — the budgetary expectation of a spurt in rural demand for fast moving consumer goods will be belied. The emergence of severe drought in several regions really made a mess of the fiscal strategy. The budget is also a product like what all CEOs bring into the market. The problem with it is that unlike what the managements of industry and business organisations have to deal with, what the Finance Minister comes up with year after year must have and, even more so, must be seen to have the widest possible favourable impact on the economy. Just as a CEO cannot expect to keep his job — with all the goodies thrown in — despite an indifferently performing product, the Finance Minister can also not hope to retain the portfolio in the face of a budget turning out to be an ineffective tool.

If we go back to the nation's history pertaining to those politicians entrusted with the demanding task of juggling with the Government's finances, only two men earlier had stayed long enough in the same post to present a succession of five Union Budgets, Dr. C. D. Deshmukh and Dr. Manmohan Singh. Their undisturbed tenure did not, however, add to their glitter. While Dr. Deshmukh had the unique distinction of orienting fiscal policy to the compulsions of plan financing and Dr. Manmohan Singh's role was no less noteworthy — tying

Government finances to the pursuit of reform — neither could claim to have been outstanding performers. Their contribution was, in retrospect, exaggerated and they were at the helm of fiscal affairs because of certain special circumstances. If Dr. Deshmukh's continued presence in the North Block had been deemed indispensable to the fate of the nation's planned development, and, likewise, Dr. Singh's unbroken innings in the Finance Ministry was seen to be critical to the success of the reform effort, this was mainly because of the two men under whom they worked. Mr. Nehru would not have any one else for the job and, as for Mr. P. V. Narasimha Rao, his own future was in jeopardy during the later part of his Prime Ministership and he could ill afford to organise a game of musical chairs for his ministerial colleagues. Mr. Yashwant Sinha also managed to present five successive budgets spread over two governments. His tenure in North Block was not spectacular in terms of fiscal policy. He was there despite the PM's preference for Mr. Jaswant Singh for the Job. This was more noteworthy than his track record.

It is but inevitable that fiscal management should have influenced the performance of industry and business, both under long years of control and under a process of reform and liberalisation. This must have been totally regardless of all the men — and one woman in the shape of Mrs. Indira Gandhi — in charge of this vital department over the years. After all, the plan outlay financed by the budget was large enough to stimulate industry and business. One must remember that the populism of Mrs. Indira Gandhi and the rural bias of Mr. Charan Singh did not hurt big business. Similarly, the professed friendliness towards industry of certain budgets did not send the corporates on a spin. The innovativeness of Finance Ministers like Mr. V. P. Singh — demonstrated in the formulation of the long term fiscal policy in December, 1985 and in the provision of a ladder instead of a lid to the small scale industries—did not achieve anything beyond some words of appreciation, that too from people who did not count.

THE ROLE OF POLITICS

In one of so many reactions to the Union Budget for 2001-2002, the concerned occupant of North Block was candid enough to concede that political factors might play a crucial role in what eventually happened. Politics had, in his innings, come in the way of his fiscal commitment to reform. On cuts in subsidies, his hands had been tied and as for privatisation, not withstanding some successes in disvestment, he did not have an easy ride. Mr. Sinha had at least managed to keep his job, given the compulsions of coalition politics, as long as he did. His predecessor, Mr. P. Chidambaram did not have such luck and the collapse of the United Front Government merely pushed him into oblivion. Mr. V. P. Singh's flamboyance, that was characterised also by the agenda for reform of the administrated price mechanism, was not enough to neutralise the repercussions of his puritanical pursuit of searches, seizures and raids against suspected tax dodgers. In the case of the present political regime, corporate lobbying was limited to the removal of the Economic Affairs Secretary, but in the days of Mr. Rajiv Gandhi it went to the extent of dictating who should not be the Union Finance Minister. Mr. V. P. Singh effectively had brought upon himself the ignomy of his removal from the North Block by his tough approach to big tax evaders. Going back to the distant past, Mr. John Mathai had to quit as Finance Minister because of his reservations about the Planning Commission and his acid remark that the mooted agency would be no more than a fifth wheel. Mr. T. T. Krishnamachari went out of the same prestigious Ministry because of the Mundra scandal, which, in retrospect, was no more than a storm in a tea cup.

4

REMEMBERING KEYNES

But, like every aspect of governance, budget making and fiscal management will inevitably have a political side. No Finance Minister can pursue an apolitical course, and necessarily has to yield to the dictates of the leader of the pack, the Prime Minister. Whatever a Finance Minister does or chooses not to do has to be partly driven by political exigencies and compulsions. There is simply no escape from this. Mr. Jaswant Singh is not the first and is not going to be the last of this distinguished member of the Government to be under political or other pressure. Anyone who is in this hot seat has to have considerable political acumen along with tactical competence. No doubt, this functionary needs more luck than his colleagues with other economic portfolios. Ultimately, this is really what decides the quality of his/her overall performance. A man like Mr. Chidambaram who followed up his presentation of a dream budget with repeated complaints that the manufacturing sector did not pass on the excise duty cuts to the buyer, obviously, was not as lucky as his fiscal give away deserved.

REMEMBERING EXPECTATION

Yet, the question is whether the Government, particularly the Finance Minister, should be so critically dependent on the sectors, which are sought to be stimulated by fiscal policy initiatives. Shouldn't a budget be good enough to succeed on its own strength? No matter whether an economy is regulated or free, whatever the Government chooses to do by way of encouragement, stimulation or correction should be duly reflected in the economy's performance. When measures are taken to instill discipline, the desired impact should be there. Likewise, the fiscal correction should achieve the intended goal. As for incentives, these should start working once the Finance Minister makes the announcement. In economics, there is a factor called expectation and Keynes was not making a fool of himself when he made this phenomenon the central aspect of *The General Theory*. In a truly free enterprise economy, expectations from whatever the Government seeks to do must bring about a normal, logical response, and this will not be dictated by the whims and fancies of intended beneficiaries. I am stressing on free enterprise only to be consistent with the basic Keynesian diktat. Even in an economy that is not free, there will be expectations, and whims leading to indifference aren't a concomitant of controls and regulations or for that matter of a liberal environment. The flop of fiscal give aways in the time of Mr. V. P. Singh and later under Mr. P. Chidambaram points to irresponsibility on the part of industry and business.

When I mention irresponsibility, I mean the business tendency to take and not give anything particularly where it is mandatory for businessmen to give. Where customs duties are cut on essential inputs and excise duties get reduced as part of an overall strategy to make the final products cheaper to the consumer, a sense of responsibility on the part of manufacturers and suppliers (meaning the distribution network) to keep their side of their side of the bargain must be glaring, not just apparent. Free enterprise should not mean a want of such responsibility. The temptation to take whatever the market can bear should not be there and must, indeed, be resisted whether or not there is an understanding between the Government on stimulating demand by way of duty cuts. Obviously, deals are made on such issues at the macro level between representatives of the Government and those of apex bodies of industry, but whatever is agreed upon between the two sides must be honoured at the level of individual manufacturers and traders.

HONOURING THE DEALS

Freedom of enterprise should not be interpreted to convey freedom from fulfillment of national level agreements. The apex bodies and various industry associations, no doubt, have to remain committed to get whatever assurances are given to Government leaders implemented at lower levels. The matter is not one of their own credibility *vis-à-vis* the Government and the interests whom they supposedly stand for. It goes beyond this limited aspect. They must assume a big stake in ensuring that the budget, and, for that matter, any major policy evolved by the Government should receive extensive support from various segments of industry and business. Such support should not be conditional on prior consultation with corporate leaders. Free enterprise should, in fact, pave the way to fostering of trust between the Government and business that everything that is done at the policy and administrative level or in plants or corporate offices is exclusively in the wider interest of the community.

Under long years of controlled economy, nobody, obviously, considered such trust necessary, since on the Government's side the statute and the enforcing authority were seen to be enough to take care of business transgressions and on the side of industry and business, the often unholy nexus with the political leadership and the bureaucracy would obviate the need for long term trust between the Government and business. In the name of promoting wider public interest and social justice, the Government introduced a plethora of controls and regulations. Virtually no commercial activity was free from the controlling hand of the Government. The industrial licensing procedure loudly declared that the politician and the bureaucrat knew more than the entrepreneur what was good not just for the latter but also for the community at large. The core sector of investment was truly awesome in terms of its classification, and it covered nearly every activity that was critical to the nation's industrialisation.

The mechanism for industrial approvals, which was part of the pompous industrial policy resolution, made it incumbent on entrepreneurs to chase the politician and official and grease as many palms as was deemed necessary to push through an industrial project. The protected market, for its part, made sure that there was no competition that could hurt. While not all projects cleared by the Government turned out to be viable, the import curbs by way of stringent quantitative restrictions and high customs duties saw to it that the products turned out found ready buyers. Inefficiency was not just tolerated. In fact, The regime of corruption, that helped sustain the licensing syndrome, signalled that lethargy and ineptness enjoyed a high premium. In such an environment, who bothered about trust and the biblical sermon about trust begetting trust? The Industrial Development and Regulation Act was primarily for all the regulation that the influential bureaucrat and the mighty politician favoured and what little development the favours the two received could condescend to allow.

TRUST AND TRANSPARENCY

Under reform, if the idea is to develop the true reform spirit, whatever had held good in a regulated economy has to give place to trust and transparency. The competitive environment must be built on battles being won strictly on merit and not on the strength of dubious deals. Thus, if a well meaning Government has come up with an offer of duty cuts to push demand, the manufacturers must fall in line. There is simply no other way out and no market player can contemplate violating a deal based on trust. The free market calls for quick reflexes, but certainly not any cheating. The consumer must be wooed and through legitimate channels and letting him down is not what the reforming economy calls for. The economics of the market place is built around several aspects of good conduct. In my sixth research study, for the IMT, *Industry and Business: Ethics and Accountability* I did concede that managers could not always behave like individuals in regard to conduct. I argued that CEOs and their teams could ill afford to ignore business-related compulsions because of ethical considerations. I voiced the opinion that where money necessarily had to pass hands, that option should not be shut out knowing that managers as good individuals would neither offer or take bribes. I accept that there should always be intellectual consistency on matters of principle. While a wrong view or reasoning should not be persisted with merely for the sake of consistency, corporates and other business organisations, I realise, have to be pragmatic and not try to emulate *Mahatmas*. Yet, such pragmatism should not extend to backing out of Government-business deals as much as wider responsibilities that are not spelt out. No CEO can assume that he or she is free to behave like the Chief Minister of Chhatisgarh on the disinvestment of Central equity in BALCO. In fact, no state Government can assume that it is bigger than the Centre. BALCO was a Central PSU and the disinvestment was not an arbitrary decision and was a recommendation of the Disinvestment Commission. Similarly, the duty cut to boost demand is a *fait accompli* and must be treated as such.

The Government-business relationship must be open and free from suspicion of any kind. Even under the most advanced form of liberalisation, the Government and various regulatory bodies will have a role in economic development. This role has to be partly stimulative and partly regulatory. Quite as important as this interventionist aspect of Governmental activity in a liberal environment would be the State's continued involvement in the development process as a massive investor. I am aware, this aspect of Indian reform has been underlined before. But, I have to reiterate this uniqueness of the Indian system since in capitalist economies Governments, while being big spenders, do not still play the kind of developmental part that we boast of. We are, no doubt, inefficient, but the Government sector, despite all its inadequacies, is the single largest player in the Indian economy. The massive provisions for the critical segments of the economy in the 2003-04 Union Budget emphasised this tellingly. In our context, the relationship between the Government and business has to be both sound and be based on mutual trust largely for this reason. The power sector continues to be dominated by the state electricity boards.

In another vital segment, banking, again, the public sector entities have an overwhelming presence. Hopefully, there will be privatisation, but going by the VSNL controversy earlier as much as the political resistance to sale of Government stake in oil sector PSUs subsequently and the fact that the banking sector still provides 40 per cent of gross bank credit to the priority sectors, it would be quite unrealistic to wish away the economic presence of the Government sector. Politicians will be whimsical and the bureaucracy will always want to show its clout and fight for its continued involvement. But, this can hardly justify irresponsible business conduct. The Indian economy deserves a fair deal and this can come about mainly through mutual trust leading to strong and growing cooperation between industry and business and Government.

A MISTAKEN CONCEPT

The market place could never have done without a heart. It was a mistake on the part of the father of economics, Adam Smith to have formulated the concept that the capitalist society was heartless and the pursuit of the profit motive was uncompromising on questions of ethics as well as welfare. Whatever he had assumed and preached on the invisible hand was unpragmatic even by the late eighteenth century standards. In fact, welfare economics did not have to emerge as different and at variance from the classical economic theory. After all, without Charles Dickens having to portray the sad tale of urchins earning the bare means of living by sweeping the chimneys, the early industrialists — the architects of the industrial revolution — should have realised that their own wealth was dependent critically on the well being of the people whom they put to work. Perhaps, such a realisation would have made the industrial revolution far more productive than it had turned out to be.

The first lesson in economics should not have been that the subject as was taught was not the same as ethics and welfare and the early students should have been told to digest the importance of both ethics and welfare to what they were learning. Anything that has to do with the market place and profit motive necessarily had to be seen and discussed in the context of a commitment to the community at large and a social consciousness on the part of all those who were gaining from the market. No business can survive for long, what to speak of flourishing. This could not have been otherwise in the early days of the industrial revolution. No business, big or small, can run by itself and on its own steam. It has to sell better and better if the goal is to grow up. For this, goodwill is a must and this explains why in book keeping a provision is made for this aspect of business. Labour has to be committed in order to be able to achieve efficiency and this commitment does not come cheap. Exploitation has never worked and never will. Participative management is much more than an academic issue. It is the essence of competitive spirit. Workers and other staff have to feel involved in whatever is done, in production, marketing and in setting goals. This is true of every organisation, from sole proprietorship to a gigantic corporate body with widespread operations.

ATTITUDINAL STRAIT JACKET

No CEO can expect wonders from just the pay cheque, that too casually given. Those who get paid have to be constantly wooed to make them deliver even in the most difficult circumstances. Big companies and small businesses alike are generally sensible enough to realise that there is ever nothing better than team work, and this is what steers organisations through hard times. The invisible hand — in the sense and the form Adam Smith had visualised it — could hardly have brought about a team that was motivated to get the best results. While the profit motive had to be the basis of entrepreneurial dynamism, sustaining it essentially demanded a team that was cohesive and was pulling in the same direction and towards a common end. Directives, policies and the norms of delegation had to be integrated to create a team that stood united even in the worst of times. The best organisation, obviously, boasted of the best team. It is well understood that the human element gets the best treatment in the infotech sector and the big strides that the latter have been making are attributed to this factor. But, the big question is why a similar treatment is not being given in other segments of industry and in the services sector. Several reasons can be advanced for this relative neglect, a narrow perception on the part of the top brass about participative management, a want of motivation of staff and an assured business environment capable of seeing the organisation through even with an attitudinal straitjacket.

It is a common tendency among managements not to wake up unless something or the other goes wrong, but they have to act, that too drastically. This was true of environment-related concerns. Till the World Bank publicly voiced these concerns in the mid-eighties, corporates did not address themselves to pollution of the atmosphere. The big multinational corporations, no doubt, were under pressure from the community and regulatory agencies alike. They sorted out their problems by dumping their polluted products in countries where environmental regulation was either weak or even non-existent. They also shifted their polluting plants wholesale to such regions. But, with growing environmental awareness worldwide, containing pollution levels to the barest minimum has become an aspect of social responsibility of business. In India, in recent months judicial activism is making up for Governmental and business apathy. But, the survival instinct is proving to be an impediment even at this juncture. You may call it the raw power of the invisible hand if you like, but there cannot, obviously, be an industry that refuses to be part of the wider community and accept the latter's rules of conduct.

TOTAL ANARCHY

The invisible hand and the profit motive surely cannot set their own rules for the manufacturers and also for the society. There will be total anarchy if this is allowed to be done. This has been brutally underscored by the wholesale fraud that became the basis of capitalism in recent years and the overstress on managerial greed in corporate management globally. It is also wrong to make business conduct the major responsibility of the regulator — this may be the Government, the autonomous authority, the judiciary or the consumer pressure group. Ideally, the invisible hand itself must be a responsible restraining and helping hand. A social consciousness and a sense of accountability must be built into the system of business management. What is needed for a system of competitive dynamism is both self-control and self-development. I am not being dismissive of regulators, but only emphasising the importance of the competitive environment being fostered by the strength as much as the discipline of the various players. Governments and courts have their roles no doubt, but not to the point where the market players fail to develop a sense of responsibility. I must emphasise this all the more in the light of all the misgovernance that has taken place in the name of business dynamism.

In the Indian context, I must accept that managements have to cope with militant trade unions, which is no easy task. Presently, the unions are powerful enough to prevent the reform process from taking a course that is imperative if the gross inefficiency and incompetence developed over the long period of socialism and State-dictated industrial management have to give way to strong and competitive efficiency. Labour management must cease to be populist and instead become totally reform-driven. Reform managements would want a clean slate, with a labour force that is manageable and accumulated losses written off. But, they are not going to get such a soft deal. They have to accept the hard realities and take these along. They have to turn glaring liabilities into healthy assets. This is what dynamic management is all about. Everything about reform is testing the business leadership, but what is management if it cannot convert tests into an advantage? The demand for a clean slate is as defeatist as that the Government must do everything in its power to prevent the invasion of the Indian market by cost and quality competitive overseas products. Gimmicks are not going to work, nor object surrender. We must witness winning management, instead of the one that wants this or that, of all people, from the politician and the bureaucrat. Legitimate policy and administrative support must be only supplementary and the real fight must come from the management itself. We can see from recent ad compaigns that manufacturers have some cushion. The various companies must pass on the cost economies to the buyer through luring prices as well as quality. That is the only course to success. Managements must negotiate with the respective trade unions ways to shed the flab. There has to be a VRS for the corporate sector for deadwood among managers, supervisors and workers. Time is running out for CEOs wherever they are. The sooner they get into the waters the better it would be for them. They have spent quite a while testing the waters. That phase is over. The the battle has begun. Let this be won.

MARKET PLACE FOR THE COMMUNITY

In this context, economics must be easy to understand and digest and should cease to be the exclusive preserve of those who claim to belong to the discipline and who are determined to keep it beyond the understanding of so many millions of people, whose life is influenced by the subject in different ways and who in turn influence it. Ultimately the market place concerns the community and *vice versa*. Neither can exist without the other. The community in its capacity as consumers outnumbers those who live on its needs and aspirations and exploit it precisely because what it wants is virtually insatiable. The invisible hand and the profit motive together constitute the mechanism of exploitation that effectively sustains the market place. Yet, there are limits to exploitation set by the maturity of the community on the one hand and by the magnitude as much as the quality of competition among those forces which are in the fray to exploit the consumers. The case for socialism and what all went in its name — State-led development and far too many curbs on freedom of enterprise—initially had rested on minimisation of such exploitation and, in fact, on promotion of public interest. Nobody then bothered about the blatant misuse of public interest, ironically in the name of fostering it. The plethora of economic legislation was justified on the ground of restraining exploitative free initiative and advancing the public good.

The politicians and bureaucrats who helped their own cause on the socialist plank expediently assumed that private enterprise necessarily went against public interest. Economists of the time, with a few exceptions, threw their lot with the socialists. It was fashionable for the academia in the fifties and sixties to consistently adopt radical postures. There were, no doubt, the pseudo intellectuals, who chose the best of both worlds — going along with the political radicals and supporting more independent causes in lieu of lucrative World Bank / IMF contracts. One must say that the World Bank's gospel of State-led growth, which dictated the development strategy of Third World countries as long as Mr. Robert McNamara was at the helm, suited them admirably. Keynes was declared irrelevant to the developing economies, and the economics of the market place received only academic attention, both literally and otherwise, since few members of the economic academia dared espouse the basics of Keynesisnism. The power of private monopolies received wide condemnation and, consistent with this radical image, most economists refused to see anything amiss in the permit-quota raj and in the latter's severity towards private enterprise. The innumerable controls and regulations on investment growth outside the public sector received wide backing and the complaint of private industry that enterprise was suffocated because of the over-stress on social justice had no takers in academic circles. Politics effectively played havoc with economics and hardly anyone minded and the virtual repudiation of the old description of economics as the science of common sense went unnoticed.

ACADEMIC STANDSTILL

Even globally there was an academic stand still until Dr. Deepak Lal came up with a blistering attack on what he derisively called the *dirigiste dogma*, representing the basis of State-led development. Dr. Lal's devastating work *The Poverty of Development Economics* (1983) had this thesis: the broad premise on which the strategy of development sponsored and controlled by the State rested was wrong in theory and practice. The euphoria that marked Dr. Lal's bitter attack on the assumptions of the Brandt Commission report did not last long and the Pak Economist, Dr. Haq used an equally strong work on the growth paradigm to come down hard on the dead economists (He left no one in doubt that he meant only Adam Smith) displacing the living economists to weaken the role of State in the development process. But, something very significant happened and that was the exit of Mr. McNamara from the World Bank and the latter's changed policy stance that development needed to be market-friendly. It is possible that pressure from the United States contributed to the World Bank playing a different tune. The *World Development Report* in the mid-eighties argued strongly in favour of developing countries becoming outward-oriented. But, even this did not push the Indian economists into the reform mould and they stuck to the radicalism of the past.

The other Brettonwood twin, the International Monetary Fund did not get caught in the ideological conflict. It remained steadfast on its loan conditionality and structural adjustment. The Fund's demands on the borrowing nations remained unchanged — the public sector (meaning the Government) fiscal deficit had to be reduced to manageable proportions, the domestic currency needed to be devalued to make the exchange rate more realistic, subsidies had to be drastically pruned etc. In retrospect, perhaps the Narasimha Rao Government in mid-1991 could have avoided full scale liberalisation when it approached the Fund with a request for balance of payment support. Or, perhaps not. One supposes, signals had been sent out that the International Monetary Fund would not settle for anything less than a reform agenda. Ever since Beijing liberalised the Chinese economy, the expectation was that New Delhi would follow suit. But, as long as Mrs. Indira Gandhi was around, it was realised that no amount of pressure would work. Apparently, some overtures were made when Mr. Rajiv Gandhi came to power, judging by his frontal attack on moneybags, the draft economic policy resolution prepared by his 'computer boys' for the New Delhi AICC session calling for liberalisation — that it got shot down because of the socialist diehards in his party, though, was not another matter — and his strong demand for reform of the public sector. When Mr. Gandhi was caught in the Bofors scandal, he inevitably retreated. The period before Mr. Narasimha Rao assumed the Prime Ministership was one in which populist politics dominated so much that developmental issues were marginalised.

In all this, the Indian economist was making no impact. In Mr. Nehru's time, Prof. P. C. Mahalanobis had seen to it that capital intensive growth models were accepted as an invaluable aspect of economic development. Under Mrs. Indira Gandhi, her mix of economic radicalism and populism overawed the academic community so much that her overtures to it quickly led to Prof. Sukhamoy Chakravorty becoming the Chairman of the Prime Minister's economic advisory council. But, there was little or no intellectual impact on whatever Mrs. Gandhi did in the economic sphere. She chose what she wanted to do and also the means. The Planning Commission was treated derisively and her son went a step further by publicly calling it a pack of jokers.

5

FROM MID-1991 TO THE PRESENT AND THE FUTURE

When Mr. Narasimha Rao opted for reform, it was largely a political decision, forced on him by a critical foreign currency assets position. The fact that as of January 18, 1991 the nation's foreign currency assets were no more than the cost of 11 days' import requirements decided that there was no other option than seeking IMF support. The agenda was set primarily by that compulsion and intellect did not matter in that game, if it was one. Obviously, it was no game since there are two equal parties — that too contestants — in any game. In the structural adjustment programme, there was no contest. If it, indeed, was one, it was grossly unequal. The substantive aspect of the programme was that there was no academic input, even from the Union Finance Minister of the time, Dr. Manmohan Singh. The intellectual infirmity became quite obvious when reform made no progress and even the rhetoric lost its strength mid-way through Mr. Rao's Prime Ministerial tenure. The lack of intellectual professionalism of members of the discipline surfaced when the advocates of control and regulation lost no time in jumping into the reform bandwagon. Those of the profession who did not get suitably accommodated duly made a noise about the neglect of poor because of liberalisation. Dr. Singh did something by way of providing a human face through enhanced outlays for social welfare programmes but, this was the politician in him that was responding to a compulsion, that was both political and administrative. Dr. Singh was also reacting as an individual embarrassed by the stark reality of the poor continuing to have a bad time.

REBUFF OF DR. LAL

It is not that Governments the world over find no use for economists who make a show of their academic accomplishments. Good economists do make an impact on policy formulation at the national as well as international level. You can see a definite link between economic thinking and international strategies. At the height of the euphoria over market-firendly development, strong support also came for a thrust on development economics and a return to the multilateral approach evolved by Mr. Robert McNamara. The 1990 global conference on development economics more than rebuffed Dr. Deepak Lal's views on the Brandt Commission's recommendations. The reputed economists who participated in the deliberations were unanimous in their view that an over-emphasis on market freedom and outward orientation could hurt the economically vulnerable sections of the community and reverse the World Bank – sponsored endeavour to lift the millions below the poverty line in the under-developed parts of the globe. Predictably, this weighty perception was not dismissed lightly and, in fact, taken seriously. Year after year, the Human Development Report put the global focus sharply on issues of human development.

Even earlier, the UNICEF in one of its forthright evaluations of the repercussions of Fund – initiated structural adjustment programme, had pleaded for reform with a human face. I must mention that the UNICEF study had quoted extensively from the staff papers of the World Bank and IMF, which highlighted how reform priorities had hindered effective poverty alleviation. The IMF has not diluted its straitjacket of fiscal and monetary devaluaton, but there is no doubt whatsoever that the borrowing countries bound by the Fund's stiff conditionality are allowed, within limits, of course, to provide for a human face to their reform efforts. The influence of welfare and development economists in this soft pedalling is unmistakable. Common with other disciplines, economics is relevant or otherwise depending on how those who are proficient in it address the day-to-day problems and even more so, the policy demands of Governments, corporate bodies and business houses. No discipline will deserve any respect if it fails to serve a useful purpose. The problem with a part of the academia is that it wants to enjoy a celebrity status without struggling for it. The rest doesn't care what it does. Obviously, it must cease to be like *Alice in Wonderland*. Who could have possibly missed this passage?

> *"Would you tell me please which way I ought to go from here?", said Alice.*
>
> *"That depends a great deal on where you want to get to", said the Cat.*
>
> *"I don't much care where – ," said Alice.*
>
> *"Then, it doesn't much matter which way you go", said the Cat.*
>
> *" – so long as I get somewhere", added Alice as an explanation.*
>
> *"Oh, you are sure to do that", said the Cat," if you only walk long enough".*

The wider goal of achieving a unique reputation is allright as far as it goes. But, nobody can take a giant leap to reach that target. There are so many small steps to take and in these, with a few exceptions, the discipline is quite as confused as Alice. If its members walk long enough, they will certainly get somewhere. But, every move must be meaningful and tactically sound. They must choose their projects carefully. They must not settle for less. Big money by itself will not enhance their reputation. Their contribution should be significant enough to win attention. Mere dialectics would not take them very far. This must be clearly understood. One must remember that for all the conceptual merit of *The General Theory*, what pushed Keynes to a pedestal was the fact that it offered a definite remedy in the aftermath of 1929 global economic depression. At the corporate level, what is needed all the time is a strategy for a specific problem or opportunity. Unfortunately, even in the so-called business schools this is not widely understood. The faculty, that supposedly prepares the managements of the morrow, often misses the wood for the trees. There have been instances of students failing to get the recognition due for their understanding of the nuances of the market place. One of them (part timers) prepared a plan that won him a promotion in the company employing him, but the reputed management institution where he was doing his MBA course declared him unsuccessful because the member of the faculty concerned wanted only a text book presentation. Effectively, the inadequacy of the teacher delayed the student's completion of the course.

A RIGID MINDSET

The economists who have been attacking the International Monetary Fund for its straitjacket were not unduly concerned about their own rigid mindset. Unfortunately, while flexibility is the demand of reform, most professions here generally refuse to look beyond their limited job-related perceptions. The auditor decides that his/her job is to find fault. The more the faults detected and reported the more satisfying is the work — this is the perception. Nothing else matters. In the wake of all the audit-related scandals that have surfaced globally in recent months, such a focus would be entirely justified, but within this the profession necessarily has to develop a versatality that is crucial for development of responsible dynamism. The accountant tries not to look beyond the books of accounts and tries not to broaden his/her perspective. Here again, despite the various accounting irregularities reported internationally, professional diligence must allow for an innovative spirit. The materials manager resigns himself to counting and recounting the inventories. The corporate buyer knows nothing about selling. The marketing wizard cannot condescend to see how the product he has to sell arrives at his door step. Yes, there is a case for specialisation, but certainly not for ignorance, more so on the ground of turning managers into specialists. While a generalist is usually favoured for the CEO's lot, as a policy, enough attention is not given to promoting along with specialisation a grasp of what all goes on elsewhere. As for the bureaucrat, he or she finds refuge in the rule book whenever he or she feels threatened by ministerial ambitions. Agreed that corporates and Government departments alike would be better off with less of yesmanship and more of constructive dissent, still those who can dare so no to the superior would be surer of evoking respect if their stance is less ideological and more pragmatic. Even where such dissent later turns out to be against the interests of the organisation concerned or the nation the dissenter would not lose credibility if his/her professionalism is not in doubt.

JESUS CHRIST AND THE DONKEY

In this context, I must recall what the former Central Vigilance Commissioner, Mr. N. Vittal said sometime ago of Jesus Christ and the donkey he rode on to spread his message of love. While the disciples of the son of God acquired knowledge by listening to his discourses, the donkey itself remained a donkey. The lesson Mr. Vittal drew from the narrative was that it all depended on the individual — acquiring wisdom or staying ignorant. The choice is for the manager, bureaucrat or the economist to make. The IAS creates generalists essentially, but nobody comes in the way of members of the service giving themselves some degree of specialisation and, along with that, the capacity to handle a variety of portfolios. But, I would not fully agree with the CVC. The bureaucrats also have to be lucky in their political superiors. Where initiative is encouraged, the young officers become motivated to give off their best. In the contrary situation that demands a servile attitude, well-intentioned officers find themselves reduced to donkeys. Mr. Vittal himself had a difficult time as Telecom Commission Chairman and Secretary, Department of Telecommunications, when Mr. Sukhram was the minister in charge. Mr. Vittal stood up to a lot of pressure on the formulation of the new telecom policy. While his professionalism was there for all to see, it is difficult to rule out the fact that Mr. Vittal had behind him a track record that most of his colleagues would have envied. It was this which gave him a tremendous advantage over Mr. Sukhram and later gave him the CVC's post.

This is true of managers and economists as well. There have been some economists who needed persuasion to join the Planning Commission and who could also turn down offers of membership of the Commission. One such member of the discipline could refuse to fall in line with Mr. Rajiv Gandhi's demand for a seven per cent plus growth in the period 1990-95. Predictably, there was another who did not need a second invitation to endorse the Prime Minister's wishful thinking. There have also been some economists who did not jump into the reform bandwagon because they seriously entertained fears about the poor getting hurt under a process of reform. But, there are also others who were prepared for compromises to get cushy jobs. The retreat by the eleventh Finance Commission from its constitutional recommendations had cast some doubts over the professionalism of its Chairman, also a reputed economist.

Developing India into a global village on its terms is easier said than done. If the village sought to be developed is based on the Indian economy getting an outside orientation more by way of being a supplier to different countries than providing an easy market to whatever comes from abroad, then, we are in for a tough ride. Over the years, the Asian Tigers acquired so much of a killer instinct as to spearhead global economic growth mainly by catering to the needs of diverse regions and countries. The success they achieved was nothing short of phenomenal. In the process, they acquired the character of global villages. When the World Bank in the mid-eighties sent the message across through its *World Development Report* about developing countries generally having to strive for an outside orientation, it wanted India to transform itself into a global village with a strong capacity to meet the growing needs of various parts of the globe. At that time, nobody here took any notice. Now, a decade and half later, we are still quite unprepared to make the effort. At the time when the World Bank made its plea the explanation came from economists that there was simply no comparison between India and Hong Kong and Taiwan. It was said that while the latter were so small and lacked a domestic market they could only export. In regard to India, the reasoning was that given its size and its huge internal market it necessarily had to be inward-oriented.

EMULATING ASIAN TIGERS

Since 1991 when the reform programme was launched, it was realised that Indian manufacturers should start emulating the Asian Tigers and that the lure of the market within would not constrain such an emulation. Economists jumped into the fray with facts showing India's meagre contribution to the global export trade *vis-à-vis* the Asian Tigers. Given the slow growth in our exports, they continue to have a case. Yet, with the reform measures of import liberalisation getting reflected in a sustained rise in the nation's non-oil import bill, our share of world exports should have at least kept pace with the rise in imports. A sense of urgency remains wanting in regard to India's outward orientation even in the face of a flooding of the local market by goods from China and South East Asian countries. There has been a lot of dynamism in the infotech sector with software exports booming and ambitious targets being set. But, the manufacturing sector is not getting into the act despite a slackening demand within forcing a slow down. The planned stimulation of the rural market by the Union Finance Minister by raising the outlay for the farm sector for the fiscal year 2001-02 and enhancing the credit allocation to the agriculture sector was virtually an acknowledgement of the manufacturing sector's limitations in respect of pushing its products into the world market. The Union Budget for 2001-02 had been silent on acquisition of an outward orientation and this was true of the two subsequent budgets as well. The long term exim policy for 2002-07 also lacked the urgency needed despite the removal of quantitative curbs on exports and a plethora of supportive measures and this was not set right by the Commerce Ministry's formulations in 2003.

Quite as important as exports to such an orientation is attracting foreign investment. Here again, comparisons have been made with China on the massive foreign investment the reformist Government has been able to secure annually ever since it decided to modernise the Chinese economy way back in 1978. A key aspect of the global village status is the level of overseas investment flow, which itself is critically dependent on the dimension of its opening up. We have not really opened up and foreign investors are yet to be convinced that India is a better destination than China. The apparent advantages — a comprehensive legal system, widespread use of the English language, a massive market potential, availability of skilled manpower, a well developed financial structure with a vast banking network as well as several non-banking financial companies and an assured supply of inputs and raw materials— have not, obviously, turned in India's favour. Rather, the informality of the Chinese system and fast clearances for investment proposals have proved too much for any MNC to overlook. The Western embarrassment over the political repression, the hostility towards Taiwan and Beijing's role in the clandestine transfer of nuclear technology to countries like Pakistan, which sponsors terrorist acts, in all fairness to China's rivals, should have neutralised the pervasive commercial liberalism practised by the communist leadership. Yet, such a neutralisation has not occurred and Beijing has had no qualms about flaunting its political record, that often borders on recklessness and irresponsibility, and still getting the support of the big U.S. corporates to the extent of the latter effectively lobbying with the White House and Capitol Hill for a lenient treatment of China's political postures.

EXCUSES WON'T DO

It would emerge from the success of China and the Asian Tigers in respect of trade and foreign investment and the indifferent performance of India that the latter has to fight very hard to globalise its economy. It would not do any more to offer excuses and explanations. The Indian economy has to offer itself as a potential global village and, not only that, make sure that the offer is accepted. But, rather than declaring that it would go the way of China and the Asian Tigers, our leadership should begin to stress on the uniqueness of the Indian economy. Yes, there are certainly aspects that are unique. Let there be no doubt about it. Our economic diplomats and negotiators do not have to be embarrassed over our large public sector, a labour force that refuses to change with the demanding times, a bureaucracy that still tends to hinder rather than promote and stimulate as it should and a political system that perpetually lets its self-interest largely decide the tenor of economic policy as well as administration. If informality is the Chinese way, there is no reason why those who are trying to sell India incorporated should be ashamed of our own system. If a former U.S. ambassador to India did not mind flying to Patna to watch how the State Chief Minister of the time was milking his cows, I do not see why we should hang our faces in shame and mortification over the Indian economy's non-Chinese characteristics.

We do not have to dump the public sector built over decades of planned development just because the pressure groups abroad do not like its face. The disinvestment process is slow-to-uncertain and in the meantime there are the so-called undertakings — it would be a misnomer to use that description—like the Bihar State Road Transport Corporation that employs on an average 86 people for each vehicle, which go on as if there is no threat to their future. (No wonder, the State Government has not paid salaries to PSU staff since 1993. The apex Court has intervened by ordering the Government to deposit Rs. 50 Crore with the Patna High Court to facilitate disinvestment of arrears, but this is no remedy to the basic malady.) The policymakers are free to reverse the socialism that was explicit in Nehruvism. But, they cannot write off the entire public sector. The loss makers, no doubt, have to be wound up, but in ways that cause the least pain to their work force. It is high time that those who negotiate with the global fraternity make this compulsion explicit. On the intransigence of the Indian trade unions also, they do not have to be apologetic. The national trade union movement grew on the basis of public interest and social justice. We reformists of today can dump the economic policy resolution at the Avadi AICC session in the dustbin of history. But, the same treatment in respect of the syndrome the resolution had given birth to rules itself out. The union leadership has to be gently persuaded to accept the rules of the reform game. The American capitalists cannot also wish away their tough unions. Even the iron lady of Britain, Mrs. Margaret Thatcher did not have everything on a platter when she decided on privatisation. The coal miners did not go down without a fight. This capitalist experience also comes handy to the Indian corporate leaders and economic negotiators from the Government side when they have to explain the constraints to the pursuit of an exit policy. I am not saying that they should take pride in our inflexible union leadership, but only cautioning against feeling ashamed of it. The banking sector, likewise, has to be defended, and not humiliated. Right, it is also refusing to reform, but the network that is truly gigantic in its spread can hardly be dismissed out of hand. Its massiveness cannot make capital adequacy and provisioning an easy proposition. We must all learn to put up a brave face, not go on saying that we are inefficient. The UTI, no doubt had made a mockery of the word 'trust', with its reckless exposure leading to a situation where it needed a massive Rs. 19,361 crore by way of support for a bail-out. But, it compared no worse with Enron and Worldcom Inc. of the United States, the functional distinction notwithstanding. All three are in the same situation of being put in the dustbin of history. While UTI has already split into UTI-I and UTI-II and has been asked by the Government to divest all subsidiary and co-promoted ventures, the American giants are still picking up the pieces.

ESSENCE OF NEHRUVISM

If India had gone the reform way in the fifties instead of building a massive public sector, perhaps it would have caused less pain than what the wholesale invasion of the domestic market by cost competitive overseas suppliers might do, if such a thing really materialises. But, with a substantial backlog of unemployed and under-employed people at the time of

Independence, no Government could have declared itself in favour of more open unemployment as a matter of policy. The political commitment to socialism did not come unprovoked in public policy. No doubt, there must have been some populism and some opportunism as well on the part of the post-Independence Government. This was natural given the strains of partition and also the demands of development. No leadership could have taken any posture that suggested insensitivity to the vast multitude of socially and economically vulnerable sections of the community. But, the irony was that Nehruvism was much more than an exercise in expediency. It was a calculated strategy to promote industrial development. Mr. Nehru was convinced that the poor would get a fair deal indirectly through socialism over period. Yet, the Government initially moved deliberately away from the essence of Gandhism to set up a number of capital goods industries covering critical aspects of growth. The Mahalanobis model formed the core of economic growth although the magnitude of poverty in the country might have been addressed better by village industries and other components of the Gandhian model. Nehruvism opted for a strategy of capital intensive development. The large public sector was expected to promote public interest. The commercial rationale in respect of employment was sacrificed, though only to a limited extent, to make it possible for the Government-owned heavy industries to absorb more manpower than they would have normally done as commercial entities. However, from the third five year plan onwards, rural development began to receive a lot of attention. This was prompted by criticism that the Mahalanobis model effectively had neglected the interests of poverty alleviation.

Now, in the context of the second generation reform it is hardly irrelevant to ask ourselves whether the adoption of Gandhism in preference to Nehruvism would have given the national economy a global competitive edge even while reducing poverty. In retrospect, while the heavy industry growth model only helped create a diverse industrial base, the socialist measure of over employment in public sector plants made the base itself lethargic in relation to the competitive forces overseas fostered under a capitalist regime. As for efforts towards uplift of the poor, neglect of efficiency considerations saw to it that these were largely blunted. When we realise that five decades after the launch of planned development the number of those below the poverty line is still considerable, we might want to rue the fact that we started reform forty years late. But, good sense demands our accepting that, late or early, we are on the course of competitive reform and also not as free agents but saddled with the burden of the past.

BURDEN OF THE PAST

This burden is no joking matter and cannot be wished away—the cumulative inefficiency of the economy, the massive backlog of unemployment and under-employment, the cost of so many postponed measures of making the different sectors and sub-sectors of the economy fitter and more productive and, above all, the cost of lethargy that dominates the Indian psyche because of a system that does not reward but often punishes initiative. It is largely this psyche that forces the more enterprising among us to look for greener pastures elsewhere. Obviously, we cannot carry this burden indefinitely. But, we cannot also dump this at one stroke. It is also the nation's sole responsibility to minimise the impact and nobody will take it from us. On how fast and how effectively we unsaddle ourselves of the dead weight depends the inherent character of India as a global village. If this burden remains, then our globalisation will take on a dimension that is contrary to the main goal of liberalisation — giving the domestic economy substantial net gains in trade and other matters. If India becomes a sitting duck for all kinds of global suppliers, the consequence could be nothing short of a disaster. Normally, exposure to the pulls and pressures of global competition should provoke a serious endeavour on our part to get rid of the various handicaps. But, the danger is that several of our manufacturers could be wiped out. This is not something that we can dismiss out of hand. We cannot have a clean slate. We all know that slums are eyesores and Mumbai can boast of — if it really would want to—the biggest slum in the whole of Asia in Dharavi that sends its own legislator and is the abode of the city's underworld. But, has anyone the courage to suggest as a policy the removal of any slum, big or small? One well known economic editor had even used his column in a national daily to speak up for the country's urban slums, citing a World Bank study in support of his arguments. That the editor of the newspaper suspended the column by way of a response was only to be expected given the general embarrassment over all the squalor that slums personified. But, the newspaper also shared the helplessness of the community in regard to an obvious blot on the urban environment.

CATS AND MICE

The embarrassment as much as the helplessness that constitute the nation's approach to slums are characteristic of the burdens that the Indian economy has been carrying. You will find that those who write or speak against the slums are also the ones who want these burdens to go lock, stock and barrel. Nothing has happened to either all this long is hardly surprising. The real issue is that neither can go on indefinitely if the economy must cease to be any longer what it should not be. The editor who exaggerated the virtues of slums relied on evidence provided by the World Bank study that the slums generated a lot of economic activity and provided considerable informal employment. The economies associated with the slums — the low cost of living and easy access to the metropolis—are by no means negligible, but to say that because of these economies the slums are critical to successful liberalisation is like saying that because we have been told since our childhood that cats live on mice the latter must multiply. That this lesson is all bunkum — since in cities both cats and mice get killed by human beings, though not devoured by them, rather than by cats and dogs — hardly makes the argument less illogical.

The economy must change and fast. It is no leopard and can change its spots. Deplorably, a decade after the start of reform, a political consensus is proving to be elusive. Now, out of power at the Centre, the Congress find it expedient to distance itself from the difficult aspects of reform. A policy document prepared for the AICC session held in March, 2001 at Bangalore virtually showed the party's embarrassment over the fact that in 1991 it was the Congress Government of Mr. P. V. Narasimha Rao which had put the Indian economy on the road to reform. The statement opposed transfer of Government ownership of profit-making PSUs and declared itself against any disinvestment preparatory to privatisaton. The argument against the Government giving up its stake to below 51 per cent in the banking sector had a familiar ring about it — that would be a reversal of the *garibi hatao* programme of the late Mrs. Indira Gandhi. If the programme should be the cornerstone of the nation's strategy on the financial sector then there would be no reform of this core segment of the national economy. On WTO arrangements, the thrust of the paper detailing what the Congress party's introspection group offered as a strategy for "sustained economic growth with social justice" was more on taking full advantage of the safeguards and "the fine print" of the basic agreements rather than as it should be on capitalising on the opportunities for free global trade available under the WTO regime. The Congress let populism and expediency cloud its earlier perception as the architect of reform when the policy document declared, "review mechanisms built into WTO arrangements must be used . . . and every care taken to ensure that the domestic economy is in no way harmed". Its retreat on reform consistent with its changed status as the main opposition party was compounded by a rhetoric that the gallery would have loved to hear: the WTO permitted tariff and anti-dumping mechanism should be used to protect domestic agriculture and industry from the fall-out of removal of quantitative restrictions on imports.

SURRENDERING TO POPULISM

Such populism was duly reflected in the stand that the Chhatisgarh Chief Minister, Mr. Ajit Jogi had taken two years back on the disinvestment of Central Government equity in

BALCO, a Centrally owned public sector undertaking located in Chhatisgarh. The Congress party's policy document circulated at the AICC session in Bangalore at that time avoided any mention of the controversy surrounding BALCO, but its choice of words left no one in doubt about its politicisation of the issue. The paper had this to say, "they (meaning the National Democratic Alliance) cannot sell the family silver — borrowing the words of the dissenting Chancellor of the Exchequer in Mrs. Margaret Thatcher's Cabinet, whom the Iron Lady promptly sacked — to meet current consumption expenditure . . . . . disinvestment proceeds should not be used to bridge budgetary gaps. These should be used to create capital assets or for investment in the social sector". Mr. Jogi chose to be much more eloquent and much less diplomatic in a newspaper article published at the height of the controversy. He was convinced that the "highest and mighty" had been party to a "sleazy" deal squandering away a profit-making PSU, estimated to be worth more than Rs. 5,000 crore, for less than a tenth of its value. Mr. Jogi raised several issues — no prior consultation with the State Government, violation of the constitutional provision against transfer of land belonging to the scheduled tribes, and, of course, what the Chief Minister called Chhatisgarh's pride. Nothing was trivial, one must accept, but then, if every time a PSU is taken up for disinvestment a host of issues is raised and a row kicked up, then this part of reform — and unsaddling of the burden of the past — is as good as dead. The Supreme Court later intervened to clear the BALCO deal, but then the judicial system is not there to speed up reform, that too at frequent intervals. The Sterlite group, no doubt, is transferring BALCO as well as another erstwhile PSU, Hindustan Zinc to a new entity. This may seem contrary to the goal of disinvestment, but Mr. Jogi cannot make too much of what those acquiring PSUs do later. After all, we are dealing with the market place.

Another State — Maharashtra — has been in a prolonged soup over its commitments to the U. S. company, ENRON, under an agreement that got under way after several hiccups. After failing to pay the power charges agreed to, the Maharashtra State Electricity Board forced ENRON to invoke the counter-guarantees. The legal consequence was that the Centre would have to shell out the State's dues. This was not all and ENRON is being replaced by another partner in the Dhabol Power Corporation. But, nothing much is happening and the impasse is seemingly endless. Yet, the fact remains that foreign investment in the power sector will come only at a price — tariffs that will guarantee the investor a commercially viable return. In any case, power rates will have to go up by a steep margin if this core sector of the economy is to get the resources which it badly needs for investment. We cannot have power being supplied almost free of cost to the farming community. The state electricity boards have been reduced to a state of bankruptcy with an oppressive populism thrust on them by way of tariffs that involve a substantial subsidy element. This anarchy has to go. The accord the Maharashtra Government had originally entered into with ENRON, more or less, set the agenda for the future of power development in the country. There is no escape from this.

A ONE SHOT DEAL

The Prime Minister offered the State Governments a one shot package for revival of the sick state electricity boards. The latter's dues amounting to Rs. 44,500 crore are being settled under the programme and the Centre is allowing states to float fresh bonds to meet the existing liabilities towards settlement of all dues by the boards to Central power entities and fuel suppliers. To facilitate redemption of the bonds, the Centre is adjusting 15 per cent of state plan funds against repayments on maturity of these bonds. The time frame has been set at two years. A major aspect of the revival programme is that there are no further Central guarantees or counter-guarantees to private power developers. Clearly, now that the deal has come into force a process of de-subsidisation has to begin. A political consensus has to emerge on commercial tariffs being charged on supply of electricity to farmers and households. It is not enough for States to sign memoranda of understanding with the Centre on the very essential — and much delayed — reforms in the electricity generation and distribution sector. The state electricity boards have to be firmly put on a commercial footing and no compromises should be allowed on their essential commercial character. It is well known that the losses of the boards are a significant component of the nation's subsidy burden. In my earlier work, *Subsidies: Piercing the Veil* (1997), I had tried to highlight the hidden and undeclared subsidies in different sectors of the economy.

A general process of de-subsidisation covering all sectors should be an aspect of the exercise of unsaddling the burden. One has to be realistic in this respect. This needs underscoring in the light of a petition filed some time back with the Nagpur bench of the Mumbai High Court, which had said that the Maharashtra State Electricity Board should pay the Dhabol Power Corporation only 89 paise per unit of electricity supplied by it. Not only that, it pleaded for a compensation from ENRON of Rs. 30,000 crore to the Union Government, the Maharashtra Government and the state board. We could do with some sanity when the tendency is to take extreme positions. Anyone in business — no matter whether this is a multinational corporation or a middle-sized domestic company — would always want to make an extra buck, but to suspect the worst is simply ridiculous. Making a profit should not be confused with profiteering and still worse, fraudulence. ENRON would have inflated some factors and deflated some others to give itself an advantage in the course of negotiations. If the U.S. multinational company did itself gain a substantial advantage, then the domestic negotiators were more to blame. The explanation that the latter did not know any of the issues related to electricity development is not acceptable since we have developed our own power infrastructure for long years. Thus, if ENRON got away with a very good bargain, this reflected very badly on the quality of those who brokered the deal. Mind you, the first agreement with ENRON was thrown in the Arabian sea and an amended one clinched. In the event of the revised deal also being a sell out — the previous record was repudiated precisely on the ground — then it is high time we honed our bargaining skills. It would not make any sense confusing our bargaining inadequacies with ENRON's mismanagement globally leading to its bankruptcy.

Returning to the wider issue of unsaddling the nation's burden, this demands parity between foreign and domestic investment. The nation has waited for a long time for a decisive measure to end the anarchy surrounding the public sector segment of the power sector. One sincerely hopes that the March, 2002 package would constitute such a measure. Ever since reform was started there has been a demand for a level playing field between foreign and indigenous players. This demand should apply as much to the incentives offered as to the consumer subsidies cut. In regard to power development, while a red carpet was rolled out to international power companies like ENRON and Cogentrix and the private power producers were given a minimum return of 16 per cent on the capital employed, the tenth Finance Commission could not go beyond projecting a return for state electricity boards of seven per cent. Ironically, even this rate is unrealistic in the face of an abysmal failure of most boards in the country to cut down their heavy losses. The subsidies on power supply to the farm sector and the households and the huge losses in transmission and distribution — currently put at 23 per cent of the total cost of generation — have received only a lukewarm political response. Try and push the same agenda on the replacement for ENRON in the Dabhol Power Corporation and you would not find anyone to take ENRON's place. If the rate of return offered to private power developers is provided to the state electricity boards, then no consumer will get a free lunch and, not only that, every user will have to pay the kind of charges that would bring about significant economies in consumption — assuming, of course, that there is no pilferage and no unmetered supply.

BEYOND THE POWER SECTOR

Obviously, de-subsidisation cannot be limited to electricity generation, transmission and distribution alone. This has to cover several other sectors, even many pockets of industry which have been exposed since mid-1991 to overseas competition in some way or the other. The small scale sector has to undergo a wholesale process of de-reservation, something that has not even started seriously. What the 1986-87 Union Budget had mooted by way of providing a ladder instead of a lid to this sector should have been the ideal way of making the constituents of this segment learn to survive without undue props. The failure of the Government to build on Mr. V. P. Singh's idea that small was not necessarily beautiful and could become so only with a fighting spirit — via a mechanism that would open up the future rather than the traditional structure that deliberately stunted growth — left small industries with an agenda for sickness and worse. While in respect of SSIs there was at least someone who thought that a change in policy was warranted, in regard to agriculture, the latter's being the biggest vote bank — though divided among different communities and castes — saw to it that the protection offered to it was only deepened with every crop season through hikes in procurement or support prices and concessional access to inputs and, what was more, no demand for its improved performance. More than ten years after the start of reform, only excuses are offered by the Government for this sector's sustained negative growth. There is no recognition yet of the urgency of competitive farm development, and protection continues to be espoused. Such a mix of complacency and expediency has to give way to a strategy that will force the true reform spirit into farms, big or small.

When I chose the caption for this part of the book *India: A Global Village?* I hardly had in mind a spread of the sluggishness, that had begun to characterise agriculture ever since the start of planned development, to the other sectors of the economy. Rather, the term village must cease to be equated with a situation of no growth and no dynamism and begin, instead, to signal quite the opposite of it. As a global village, India — meaning all its economic segments — must provide the drive to the global economy in the same way that the small Asian Tigers have done. Obviously, despite apprehensions voiced of the domestic economy being overwhelmed by goods of cheaper and more quality conscious producers and manufacturers elsewhere, we lack the import potential to be able to influence the growth of world trade even by the smallest of margins. With our limited export competitiveness, there is also no question of our producers and manufacturers doing the tigerisation act. Those who did speak loudly of India's impending tigerisation at the height of the liberalisation euphoria have stopped entertaining such sentiments about India's progress under reform. Quite some time ago, the realisation had hit the zealous supporters of India's opening up initiatives that indigenous enterprise could never match the buoyancy of the Asian Tigers.

Yet, after the removal of all quantitative restrictions on the inflow of merchandise, the nation has been left with no alternative other than to fight the assault on Indian products and goods through a counter assault on our competitors, those who have emerged strongly and those who are emerging. We must meet aggression with aggression. For this to become a strong policy instrument, it is incumbent on politics to yield to economics. Every act of disinvestment of Government stake in public sector undertakings must be completed expeditiously. Political forces must stop readily assuming that they inevitably have a substantial stake in whatever the Government seeks to pursue in this part of the reform process. Likewise, de-subsidisation must go on smoothly without some party or politician kicking up a row for shortsighted political gains. Five decades after the start of planned development in this far flung nation, nobody can realistically and justifiably complain of our being pressurised by the Americans and the World Bank / IMF to make the domestic economy perform on terms of parity with the best players in the world. If at all any pressure has to be mounted, this has to be done by ourselves. Indeed, the reform task is entirely ours. What happened in 1991 is irrelevant to our accepting full responsibility for completing the large unfinished reform agenda.

CONCLUSION

I have once again come up with several ideas on the future of the Indian economy. Long years of State-led development and a protected market had accustomed various sectors and the players in them to a style of functioning that showed little or no urgency about the tasks that lay before them. Although reforms were initiated in mid-1991, still in the decade and more that has gone by, there was no evidence of a positive change in attitudes. While fears were voiced and demands made for what was called a level playing field for Indian players, there was little preparedness for a competitive environment.

I have tried to define the kind of role that India should play — what sort of a global village it should be. I have asked myself whether the Indian economy can tigerise itself and acquire a truly outward orientation. I am aware that my perceptions cannot decide the status of India as a global player. Yet, intellect is not always far removed from the hard realities. What I have said in this part of the book would have served the intended purpose if only the various sectoral players begin to perform as global competitors and with a vision that goes beyond the limited local market. Their task is to sell more and more abroad and simultaneously to prevent their being overwhelmed by suppliers from abroad. The long term exim policy for 2002-07 has set the procedure right for the export effort. But, the battle has to be fought by the players themselves.

Part—II
ISSUES OF MANAGEMENT

IN PERSPECTIVE

Management is largely an exercise in creating positive human responses. One person's positive approach invariably provokes a similar attitude among others. Likewise, when someone has a negative mindset he or she is certain to create an equally destructive sentiment among those coming into contact with him or her. Sometime ago, an institution of repute honoured four employees who had completed 20 years of service. The function organised on the occasion set me thinking. I wondered about the role the institution should play in promoting such a sense of loyalty. In a dynamic environment, jumping jobs is only to be expected and it may even be considered unprofessional to question the dedication of a person who keeps on looking for better and more challenging career opportunities. Still, organisations flourish on the strength of people who decide to swim with them whatever happens rather than perpetually looking for alternative positions.

The Indian economy has now been under a process of liberalisation for nearly a decade and there is a growing demand for adoption of the capitalist practice of hire and fire. Obviously, no organisation can tolerate laggards or also rans, and the Indian economy didn't have to wait for the start of the reform period to recognise this essential aspect of good management.

The question is how we can reconcile the virtue of loyalty among staff with the compulsions of running institutions in an increasingly competitive environment. Obviously, there can be no case for tolerating inefficiency in the name of rewarding loyalty. A person, who chooses to stay in one organisation must be doing something worthwhile to merit his or her retention. When we say this, we assume that judgements are not made subjectively and the contribution of employees is measured objectively and fairly.

I am not comfortable with the superior-subordinate relationship, a view that I had expressed in my best seller *Power of Motivation* (1993). Ten years later, I am convinced that this warrants reiteration. The preference clearly is for the team spirit. In fostering this spirit everyone has a role and no person is either too small or too big. Loyalty must go hand in hand with professionalism and both must be pervasive.

—K.S. Ramachandran

THE LAUNCHING PAD

MANAGEMENT OR MISMANAGEMENT?

The essence of managerial excellence lies in achieving success as much as in avoiding failure. Managing a business or non-business organisation is no exercise in soft options and decision makers must be ready all the time for any eventuality—capitalising on a half chance, as cricketers know it, to make a substantial gain or doing the fire fighting if the situation so warrants. I could have called this part of the publication the Free Speak on Mismanagement to give it the provocative launch it needed. The provocation notwithstanding, such a title could have given it a sense of purpose considering that the global record of management is partly one of depressing flops and that there have only been a few great victories. I feel compelled to say this after the excesses committed by corporate bosses in the United States, forcing the Bush Administration to come down hard on CEOs of all mega companies.

Books on management have generally tended to focus on titans who made success a habit and glossed over lesser mortals who either carried on in a pedestrian manner or gave up in the face of daunting challenges. But, the experiences of a few corporate barons have no great relevance to the market place and specifically to under-performers. The market is constantly demanding and nothing but the best will do when pressure is really mounting.

The small men and women with no pretensions are the ones whose track record will make some sense to the brats wanting to become barons. For, geniuses are rare and the market is full of managers who are always unsure of how the business environment will behave and how they should conduct themselves. When they are able to get their act together and either avert a crisis or make some gains while the going generally is bad, they deserve to stand up and be counted.

Business has never known chivalry and will never know it. There are deeds of valour that characterise successful businessmen but hardly any of them can ever boast of chivalry. One's food is another's poison and *vice versa* and successes are often achieved at the expense of others. Those who want to surge ahead must be looking constantly at their strong points as much as the Achilles heels of their potential or existing rivals.

There are laws everywhere to prevent business-related excesses, but those at the top might have reached their positions largely on the strength of practices, which were perilously close to what the statutes specifically sought to prevent. Yes, successes in the market place are built more often than not on the power of exploitation of one kind or another. Left to themselves, scruples may not always be for corporate chiefs who want to move up the ladder and fast. For them, business and ethics may not always mix.

Yet, the market cannot and should not be divorced from the community at large and business must respect the essence of ethics. Corporate policies and practices must seek to combine commercial prowess with social accountability and orderly functioning, meeting the kind of agenda that President Bush of the United States has set for the giant corporations in response to the recent spake of scandals. This, indeed, should be the basic programme of management generally. The concluding part of the book endeavours to promote such a programme. I rightly decided to leave the task to people engaged in diverse fields. The contributors have in different ways lent strength to my visualisation of India as a global village. As I had anticipated, the two parts have combined to make a serious intellectual exercise.

—K.S. Ramachandran

6

MANAGING ISN'T A CHANCY AFFAIR

—K.S. Ramachandran

Whether one likes it or not, the balance sheet is what ultimately decides how well or badly managers perform. The fate of the balance sheet, however, does not depend entirely on a single minded managerial pursuit of profit making as the strategic goal. Profit earning depends on varied actions and these need not as a rule be related. There are always fortuitous factors at work, over which even the best corporate or non-corporate strategist has little control. But, this does not mean that managing is necessarily a chancy affair. An effort — a serious one at that — should be made to anticipate and prepare for every eventuality. Managers should do everything that they can to put themselves and the organisations they run firmly on the road to success. What they do should be very well planned and there should be no compromise on this aspect of management.

EXCELLENCE IN MANAGEMENT

Excellence in management is achieved by good planning and still better implementation of the plans drawn up. Economics, contrary to what text books lay down, is neither a matter of chance nor casualness. Supply and demand, the two core elements of performance, test managerial skills as nothing else can and the battle plans have to be constantly focused on these factors. Demand does not always push supply as is conveniently assumed and the best performers in the market place do successfully push demand by way of supply. The best brands of today are those that are not demand-led but pulled and pushed alike by supply. When tastes are constantly changing, it is tactically necessary to create a new demand by offering a product or a service that seeks to meet an unfelt need or provide a satisfaction that is somewhere beneath the surface.

Economics has never been a joke and will never be one. The first lesson in successful management is to understand this quickly enough and to act upon this understanding before anyone else does. In a fiercely competitive environment, the one who shoots first gets everything and the rival who is slow in drawing the gun loses. In the corporate world, a lot of espionage goes on and it is hard to keep business secrets. Development of a new product has to be closely guarded. This caution applies equally to buy-out deals and mergers and acquisitions. With growing computerisation, secrets are not easy to keep and a managerial team which is preparing to spring a surprise on its counterpart in a competing enterprise may find itself at the receiving end of a bigger and more unpleasant surprise.

VIRTUAL REVOLUTION

On matters of supply and demand, the emergence of a virtual revolution has in turn led to a situation where a calculated move of one corporate is overtaken quickly by the tactical game of a rival. A virtual product, obviously, cannot be kept for long at the planning stage and must be on the shelf ready to be picked up by the customers before a better option is available to the prospective buyer. But, speed should never get equated with haste and dynamism should never deteriorate into either shortsightedness or clumsiness. After all, the market has never accepted also rans and is less likely to do this in the present context of one-upmanship. Managers must know what their rivals are doing but should ensure that the latter have no clue to what they themselves are contemplating. Espionage should benefit them and hurt their competitors instead and even maim them. Dominance of the market has to be the ultimate goal and this can be achieved only by routing those who pose an impediment or at least effectively marginalising them.

Admittedly, free competition is the declared norm, but success in business means stifling competition. This explains why lawmakers nearly everywhere have provided for ways to control those who seek to dominate and to help those who want to succeed without impeding the progress of others. But, those who are determined to reach the top would not want to be constrained too much by ideals that are moved by social justice-related considerations. They know that their ambitions will put them on a collision course with anti-monopoly forces, but managing these forces is also part of the overall game of winning. Broadly, there are only two choices at the market place — winning or losing — and those who have success as their overriding aim will have to constantly focus on winning. Those who cannot fight to win would be better off being outside the market place and doing something other than dirtying their hands with running enterprises in business and industry, as Peter Drucker would have put it.

7

PETER DRUCKER's GOSPEL

Management's new dimension

When something is written or spoken on management it is but inevitable that the inspiration for this should come from the writings of management gurus. Here I seek to share with readers what Peter Drucker had said in "The Frontiers of Management" (1986) on social innovation, which he called the management's new dimension.

My last example of social innovation is management. "Managers," of course, have been around a long time. The term itself is, however, of twentieth-century coinage. And it is only in this century, and largely within the last fifty years, that management has emerged as a generic function of society, as a distinct kind of work, and as a discipline. A century ago, most major tasks, including the economic task we call business, were done mainly in and by the family or by family-run enterprises such as the artisan's small workshop. By now, all of them have become organised in institutions — Government agency and university, hospital, business enterprise, Red Cross, labour union, and so on. And all of them have to be managed. Management is, thus, the specific function of today's "society of organisation". It is the specific practice that converts a mob into an effective, purposeful and productive group.

Management and organisation have become global rather than Western or capitalist. The Japanese introduced management as an organised discipline in the early 1950s and it became the foundation for their spectacular economic and social successes. Management is a very hot topic in the Soviet Union. And two of the moves of the Chinese after the retreat from Maoism were to set up an enterprise management agency in the Prime Minister's office and import an American-style management school.

FROM THE TRADITIONAL TO THE MODERN

The essence of modern organisation is to make individual strengths and knowledge productive and to make individual weakness irrelevant. In traditional organisations — the ones that built the pyramids and the Gothic cathedrals — or in the armies of the eighteenth and nineteenth centuries, everybody did exactly the same unskilled jobs in which brute strength was the main contribution. Such knowledge as existed was concentrated at the top and in very few heads.

In modern organisations, everybody has specialised and, fairly advanced, knowledge and skill. In the modern organisation, there are the metallurgist and the Red Cross disaster specialist, the trainer and the tool designer, the fund raiser and the physiotherapist, the budget analyst and the computer programmer, all doing their work, all contributing their knowledge, but all working towards a joint end. The little each knows matters; the infinity each doesn't know does not.

The two cultures of today may not be those of the humanist and the scientist as C.P. Snow, the English physicist-turned novelist, proclaimed thirty years ago. They may be the cultures of what might be called the *literati* and the managers. One sees reality as ideas and symbols and the other sees reality as performance and people.

Management and organisation are still primitive. As is common in every rapidly evolving discipline — as was true, for instance, in medicine until fairly recently — the gap between the leading practitioners and the great majority is enormously wide and is closing but slowly. Far too few, even of the most accomplished of today's managers in all organisations, realise that management is defined by responsibility and not by power. Far too few fight the debilitating disease of bureaucracy — the belief that big budgets and huge staff are accomplishments rather than incompetence.

AN EMPLOYEE SOCIETY

Still, the impact has been enormous. Management and its emergence have, for instance, rendered equally obsolete both social theories that dominated the nineteenth century and its political rhetoric: the Jeffersonian creed that sees society moving towards a crystalline structure of independent small owners — the yeoman on his forty acres, the artisan in his workshop, the shopkeeper who owns his own store and the independent professional —and the Marxist theorem of a society inexorably turning into an amorphous gas of equally impoverished, equally disenfranchised proletarians. Instead, organisation has created an employee society. In the employee society, blue-collar workers are a steadily shrinking minority. Knowledge workers are the new and growing majority — both the main cost and the main resource of all developed societies. And although knowledge workers are employees, they are not proletarians but, through their pension funds, the only capitalists and, collectively, the owners of the means of production.

It is management, which in a large measure accounts for this century's most extraordinary social phenomenon — the educational explosion. The more highly schooled people are, the more dependent they then become on organisations. Practically all the people with schooling beyond high school in all developed countries — in the United States the figure is 90 per cent plus — will spend all their working lives as employees of managed organisations and cannot make their living without them. Neither can their teachers.

8

NO ROOM OR NEED FOR CLASS CONFLICT

—Mritunjay Athreya

Management worldwide, especially in new entrants to the globally freer trade arena like India, should focus on the following: First, offering winning value propositions to customers, in order to retain those existing and attract new ones and satisfy as well as delight all of them. Secondly, creating high economic value to reward existing shareholders, at any given point, and attract new investors and lenders. Thirdly, designing organisations to attract, retain, develop and utilise talent. Fourthly, building a long-term partnership with vendors, dealers and other business associates. Fifthly, providing good corporate governance, upholding law, ethics and social responsibility.

ROLE OF COMPETITIVE QUALITY

The calibre of the management team is a key determinant of the competitive quality of corporates. The market enables most corporates to access funds, equipment, materials etc. But, it is their effective deployment and utilisation that can really create competitive advantage. The contribution of management includes the creation of a shared vision; longer term strategic plans; timely commitment of investments in capacity,

Dr. Athreya is a reputed management consultant

technology, brands and HRD, short term planning, scheduling, information, monitoring and control systems; goal setting, performance appraisal, compensation, coaching, rotation and development of talent; internal and external communication; employee relations; and boundary management. Above all, management has to provide inspiring and transformational leadership.

There is a mistaken notion that higher quality inevitably involves higher cost. One of the *mantras* in quality is that quality costs nothing. If at all, it lowers costs by reducing rejections, re-work and other forms of waste. In fact, ensuring quality can improve profits and profitability. For example, an improved quality of design, vendor development and buying will reduce material mix, prices and inventory costs for a specified level of quality, to meet customer expectations in the chosen segment and price category. Similarly, an enhanced quality of equipment maintenance and operation will reduce the cost of downtime and repairs. Use of not only statistical quality control but also statistical process control will improve the reliability of the process and ensure better quality, uninterrupted, longer runs and, hence, lower costs. So, it is not quality vs. cost but quality plus.

COMBATIVE MANAGEMENT

The simultaneous impact of liberalisation, globalisation and privatisation is to make competition fiercer. In that context, managers not only will be but have to be combative, in the sense of being proactive, aggressive and taking the battle to the other camp. Examples of combative management are pre-emptive expansion of capacity; first to introduce new products; contribution pricing; restructuring; rightsizing; acquisition; merger; demerger; divestment; dropping unprofitable divisions, locations and products; and letting go chronically low performing vendors, dealers, executives and workers, etc.

Management should stress the community of interest not only between the internal stakeholders of employees, management and promoters, but also between them and the external stakeholders — customers, investors and the society. There is no room or need in the new paradigm for class conflict. In a sense, all are employees or, better still, associates or members of the business institution. They are co-trustees, earning their just rewards by serving the external stakeholders. They should practise self-governance through high performance, propriety and systems, thus, making board governance easier.

MANAGING IN THE NEW MILLENNIUM

—S. Neelamegham

Though we are three years into the new millennium, we are still on the threshold of a new global age. Under the impact of globalisation, more and more of the national economies are being integrated with the global economy. Markets are becoming global not only for goods but also for many services. World trade is expanding at a blistering pace. Financial markets are getting increasingly interconnected. No wonder, developments in these markets in recent months have been the most dramatic. It is now estimated that an average $500 billion cross the world's foreign exchange markets each day, a major portion of which may be quite unrelated to trade or investment. Further, information technology has become a powerful force and is shaping the new knowledge economy. An increasing number of developing countries are removing trade barriers, dismantling capital controls, encouraging foreign investment and opening up their economies.

These developments have drastically altered the landscape. Economic boundaries are being redrawn and a borderless world is fast emerging. With the presence of transitional companies in domestic markets, competition is getting intensified. Thanks to media explosion, there has been a convergence of global

Dr. S. Neelamegham has served as Professor of Marketing and Dean, Planning and International Relations, University of Delhi.

consumer preferences for many products and services. Global branding and advertising and cross border buying and selling have more or less merged. To meet the challenges of global competition; large, medium and small companies are entering into strategic alliances with corporate giants to exploit jointly the global markets by offering superior quality products and services. It is increasingly realised that in future only those companies, which have developed products of global standards, will be able to retain their market share and achieve growth and profits.

GLOBALISATION—THE CORPORATE RESPONSE

Globalisation is the corporate response to the requirements of the fast changing global business environment. This response has been vastly aided by the structural adjustment programmes pursued by both developing and developed countries. With the growing trend towards liberalisation and transformation of more and more of the regulated or guided economies into market economies, 'One World, One Market' is no longer a distant dream but is fast becoming a reality. Globalisation of trade, liberalisation of the economy and growth of foreign direct investment help corporations to interact globally through joint ventures, mergers and acquisitions to improve their global competitiveness. Corporations are able to set up a multinational network of information, research and production across borders. This in turn enables them to upgrade, absorb, adapt and innovate technologies, which hold the key to global competitiveness. And this leads to greater integration of national economies with the global market place. Globalisation benefits all economies including the low-income developing countries. As a result of integration with the global economy, domestic firms get the opportunity to participate in international production of goods and services and are able to increase their presence in global markets.

PROBLEMS AND CHALLENGES OF GLOBALISATION

While globalisation provides new opportunities, it also carries with it many risks. The founder of the World Economic

Forum, Mr. Klaus Schwab and its Managing Director, Mr. Claude Smadja, some time ago had observed that:

- Economic globalisation was causing severe economic dislocation and social instability.
- The technological changes of the past few years had eliminated more jobs than they created.
- The global competition that was part and parcel of globalisation led to winner-take-all situations; those who came out on top won handsomely, but the losers were worsted.
- Higher profits no longer meant greater job security and better wages. Globalisation tended to delink the fate of the corporation from the fate of its employees.
- Unless serious corrective action was taken soon, the backlash could turn into open political revolt that could destabilise the Western democracies.

At the same time, Mr. Schwab and Mr. Smadja had argued that the globalisation process was irreversible and that the task for political and economic leaders was to demonstrate how the new global capitalism could function to the benefit of the majority— and not only for the corporate managers and investors — and convince the general public that the current economic restructuring would lead to renewed prosperity. They favoured a focus on training and education, the constant overhauling of telecommunications and transportation infrastructure, entrepreneur-promotional fiscal policies and on recalibrating social policies to increase national competitiveness.

EAST ASIAN CRISIS—THE END OF AN ERA

In the mid 90s, the East Asian countries were often cited as examples of successful countries which benefited from trade liberalisation and export-led industrialisation and growth policies. Their openness to the world economy, pursuit of an export-oriented development strategy, liberalisation of foreign trade regimes, adaptability of their labour force and

Governmental commitment to coherent policies towards liberalisation across different sectors of the economy were cited as major factors contributing to their extraordinary economic performance. It was believed that the Asian miracle was the shining light whose example would be followed by many other developing countries and that it would greatly contribute to growth of the world economy. However, the second half of 1997 shattered these hopes. The East Asian stock market collapsed. Currencies crashed. Enterprises failed. The rapid growth of the past turned into recession. There was a slow down in exports. And this affected not only other Asian economies but also the world economy. Pessimists readily declared that the Asian miracle was a myth and could be the beginning of the end of globalisation.

There are several lessons to be drawn from the experiences of East Asian countries. Firstly, the financial crisis in East Asia had underlined the need for Governments to make public accurate and timely economic information. It highlighted the need for sound macro-economic management along with micro economic efficiency in regard to the financial system of every country. Secondly, banks must be prevented from building up risky short-term liabilities especially denominated in foreign currencies. Thirdly, deployment of funds borrowed abroad for consumption or misguided investment in real estate was risky. Fourthly, prudential supervision of domestic financial systems, commitment to good governance and accurate as well as transparent financial reporting had become essential. Last but not the least, economic policies and programmes had to meet country-specific situations if they were to be effectively implemented.

The collapse of East Asian markets only marked the end of an era but certainly not the end of globalisation. All the developing countries, whether they are in Asia, Africa or elsewhere, continue to depend on foreign technology and investment. The greatest change in the world economy since the Second World War has been the extent to which it has gone international. Trade, services trading and financial markets have turned global. It is, therefore, not possible for any nation to live in isolation in a world which is becoming increasingly integrated.

TECHNOLOGY- AN INTEGRATING FORCE

The world economy of the new millennium as it progresses will be shaped greatly by technological developments. The rapid technological advances in transport and communication and the emergence of several key industries — microelectronics, biotechnology, telecommunications, robotics and computers — would continue to play a major role in integrating the world economy. For example, the advantages inherent in microelectronics have already accelerated worldwide communication providing the foundation for the emerging global society. Technology leads to social change and development. Since the eighteenth century, a series of technological innovations transformed agrarian into industrial societies. When the telephone, transistor, radio, television and the satellite network are combined with the on going technological advances, the world will be on the verge of yet another profound transformation. Information technology would propel a regime where knowledge would become power and information wealth.

Internet is now a massive reality., According to Forrester Research, e-commerce has grown from $4.8 billion in 1998 to $327 billion in 2002 in the United States alone. In the case of India, there are over 1.5 million users while the volume of business done on e-commerce exceeds Rs.2,500 crore. According to a NASSCOM forecast, the business will grow to over Rs.10,000 crore by 2020. The current trend is towards convergence and consolidation. Computers and networking have made it possible to have a digital community. According to Nicholas Negroponte, one of the world's foremost experts on multimedia, "in this millennium your right and left cuff links or earrings may communicate with each other by low orbiting satellites and have more computer power than your present PC. Your telephone won't ring indiscriminately; it will receive, sort, and perhaps respond to your incoming calls like a well-trained English butler. Mass media will be redefined by systems for transmitting and receiving personalised information and entertainment. Schools will change to become more like museums and playgrounds for children to assemble ideas and socialise with other children all over the world. The digital planet will look and feel like the head of a pin."

DEMOGRAPHIC SHIFT

Another major force that is going to make the world of the new millenium different is the trend in population growth. The population of the world, which is currently over six billion, will reach eight billion by the year 2020. But, almost 95 per cent of the increase in population will take place in the developing countries. Thus, there will be an over-populated developing world and an under-populated developed world, causing demographic imbalances between richer and poorer countries. Also, the developed world will have more aged people. When these changes occur simultaneously with sweeping technological changes, these are likely to pose several new challenges to developing countries. Physical resources may become short in supply and developing countries may be unable to cope with the new problems related to environmental degradation.

The globalisation of financial systems and services has brought in its wake several new challenges to the nation state. The borderless world implies that the Government has less control over its currency and fiscal policies compared to what it had in yesteryears. In future, Government may become smaller still, leaving many of the business functions to the corporate sector. Industrial policies in several countries are already being reshaped. There is a steady shift away from Government interventions to protect home industries to conditions aimed at improving economy-wide competitiveness. Restructuring, disinvestment and privatisation of public enterprises are gaining greater importance. In respect of developing countries, the Government will have to design policies and programmes necessary to take care of those likely to be adversely affected because of deregulation and a change over to the market economy. The Government may have to play a key role in evolving appropriate strategies to ensure that the benefits of globalisation reach the poorer and weaker sections of the society and also take steps to eradicate poverty, unemployment, ignorance and squalor.

FUTURE OF GLOBAL TRADING ENVIRONMENT

A new vision had emerged with the establishment of the World Trade Organisation in 1995 to bring together trading partners and achieve a multilateral economic framework covering many areas common to the world economy. At the same time, the growth of powerful trade blocs in the international economy created apprehensions about new forms of protectionism. In July 1997, the European Commission had presented the agenda 2000. It took a historic decision to further strengthen the European Union by opening the doors to central and eastern European countries. The first accessions took place in 2003. The agenda included reform of regional aid as well as the common agricultural policy, and enlargement and financing of the EU for the period 2000-2006. The European Union is the biggest market in the industrialised world with a population of over 370 million and a world trade share of about 20 per cent. Similarly, the conclusion of the North American Free Trade Agreement (NAFTA) and the formation of APEC present major challenges to several developing countries especially in Asia and Africa, which entertain the fear that they might be left out of the world trade development mainstream. Further, while pressure is put on developing countries for greater liberalisation and opening up their economies, it is feared that developed countries might use trade as a weapon through their insistence on the social clause, including labour and environmental standards.

ENVIRONMENTAL ISSUES

There is no doubt that with growth in population and depletion of natural resources, there would be a growing thrust on environmental issues and challenges in the coming decade. The meeting on Agenda 21 of the UN Environment and Development held at Rio sometime ago reflected a broad — even tentative — consensus on several issues to be tackled for providing better protected and managed ecosystems and integrated development programmes. Promoting clean production, giving responsible entrepreneurship, contributing to sustainable development, enhancing research and development of environmentally sound technologies and environmental management systems, fostering ethical management of products and processes and taking measures for bringing about an increased environmental awareness among employees are some of the responsibilities, which business and industry will have to take up in the coming years. While it is true that adoption of environmentally friendly technologies and production processes will, in the long run, provide opportunities to improve their sales to environmentally conscious consumers, firms in the developing countries are going to face several issues and challenges as they have to incur heavy costs at least in the short turn, which might affect their competitiveness.

In a global economy, where the different economies interpenetrate one another in large part through trade and investment, the foremost requirement is that Indian business and industry must improve their global competitiveness. They must develop their capacity to compete with the rest of the world on equal terms. They must be forward looking if the competitive challenges are to be met on the export front. Their focus should be on upgradation of technology, strengthening R&D, improving quality standards and providing responsive customer service as well as cost effectiveness. Striving for and maintaining a strong competitive position in world markets should become their goal.

COMPETITIVENESS AND EXPORT STRATEGY

The experience of East Asian countries suggests that unless we improve our export performance we cannot sustain economic growth. China' s merchandise exports had risen from $8.1 billion in 1980 to $148.8 billion in 1995 whereas India's exports rose from $8.6 billion in 1980 to a mere $30.8 billion over the same period during the next seven years, while China marched faster India lagged well behind despite an impressive performance in fiscal 2002-03. It is time that we revamped our export strategy and removed the various obstacles to rapid export growth. A stable exchange rate, a modest current account deficit, removal of procedural hurdles and improving infrastructure facilities are all required for creating an environment conducive to accelerated export growth.

Also, there is need to bridge the knowledge gap. In the new millennium, knowledge workers will play a decisive role in determining a firm's competitiveness. More than the physical assets it is the human capital of the company, which will play a major role. So, corporations will have to provide for a much higher level of investment in the selection, training and development of their personnel with the requisite skills as the new knowledge replaces the old.

Besides, corporations will have to restructure their organisations to ensure a faster response to the changing demands of global consumers. To achieve increasing productivity as well as organisational efficiency, they have to make their organisations more flexible and adaptable in tune with the varying requirements. With the development of an information network and the growing number of knowledge workers, organisations will tend to become flatter instead of continuing to have a traditional hierarchical structure. Companies will have to embrace the concept of relationship marketing and win consumers for an entire lifetime. With accent on e-commerce, companies will have to develop a new marketing model that helps to attract customers, learn about preferences and build brand loyalty through "customer delight".

In future, trade, investment and fund flows will be largely influenced by regional trade blocks. Corporate managers can no longer consider only nation states. Their decisions on marketing, manufacturing and investment will have to transcend national boundaries and their impact on the needs and aspirations of trade blocks will have to be reckoned with. The role of the State is changing and that of the Government is being redefined the world over. The place of State as a prime economic agent and as a producer of goods and services is declining. In the global economy, the performance of the Government is judged by the way it controls the fiscal deficit and manages its budget and tax administration as well as facilitates economic growth in general. A sound economic policy and an efficient and market-friendly Government are essentially needed to attract foreign investment, which itself is emerging as the driving force for our economic growth. This not only calls for improvement in public sector management but also a wholesale reinvention of the Government.

STATE'S ROLE DIMINISHING

It is realised, however, that the State's role as a regulator of the financial system and economic services and its part in regard to social obligations will in no way diminish nor is there going to be a conflict between globalisation and the State's discharging of these obligations. This is very succinctly expressed by the Nobel laureate, Dr. Amartya Sen when he says in the context of India: "...much more is involved in freeing the Indian economy from the cage in which it has been confined, and many of the relevant tasks call for more — not less — Government activity and public action". While he agrees with the need to avoid a counter-productive role for the State in controlling business and industry, he calls for positive Government intervention in regard to areas like basic education, health care, social security, land reform and promotion of social change.

The challenge, therefore, is how to create an efficient economy, which will liberate not only business and industry from the various rules and regulations that have so far stifled economic growth but at the same time would strengthen the hands of the Government to discharge its social obligations more effectively and efficiently. The new era of globalisation provides opportunities as well as challenges. Closer linkages and integration of economies provide opportunities for economic growth, trade development and for improving the living standards of the people. In order to avail of the benefits of the new knowledge economy, we must have the courage to think globally, to break away from the traditional paradigms and plunge boldly into the unknown. The task is to design and implement bold policies — with emphasis on effective mobilisation of resources, sustained exports, foreign investment, human resources development, strengthening competitive advantages, protection of the environment, social justice and a determination to integrate with the global economy—to facilitate India' s entry into the world of tomorrow, where there will be no poverty and misery and "where the mind is without fear and the head held high, and where the world has not been broken into fragments by narrow domestic walls."

10

NOT AS COLLABORATORS BUT AS GRABBERS

—D.H. Pai Panandiker

In the first flush, the reforms were unreservedly welcomed. But, when the hard facts had to be faced, business began to grumble and finally advocated a slow down if not reversal of some of the measures undertaken by the Government. That was because business and some sectors of industry were quite unprepared for what was to follow. That was a big challenge, which, if squarely faced, could have turned every problem into an opportunity. Reforms brought up various problems from two directions. First, the reduction in quantitative restrictions opened the floodgates for imports of a variety of commodities Initially, these were restricted to capital goods, raw materials and components. Effective April 1, 2001, all quantitative restrictions were removed and the various goods subjected only to tariff. The rate of tariff has also been brought down. This has made foreign goods cheaper and intensified the competition with domestic industry. Unless domestic industrial enterprises are able to increase productivity and bring prices down, they will be wiped out. So far, almost all have survived because there was simultaneously a fall in the value of the rupee. Protection, ironically, took a different form from what industry enjoyed earlier.

Dr. D.H. Pai Panandiker is Advisor, RPG Enterprises & President, RPG Foundation. He was formerly Secretary General, FICCI.

POSING A THREAT

Another source of concern was the growing competition from foreign companies in India. They no longer came as partners and collaborators but as market grabbers. Their presence in infrastructure was welcomed but in the manufacturing sector this was resented. Even some of the old partners were not content to continue with the relationship and wanted to hold majority shares in the joint venture companies. The only alternative was to sell out the holding for which, however, a few of the Indian promoters were prepared. In the area of durable consumer goods, a number of enterprises have been taken over by the foreign partners. Coca-Cola, Whirlpool and Daewoo have bought over Indian equity and are posing a threat to other companies in the concerned sectors.

It is against this background that managements of Indian companies have to devise new strategies to survive and progress. The dimensions of business have changed. Every enterprise has to take into consideration the possibility of competition coming from anywhere in the world. This has put every enterprise on the alert, a situation that was not visualised during the heydays of industrial licensing. At the same time, the market for diverse products has enlarged considerably and, if an enterprise plays its cards well, it can grow without limit. Several companies in software like Wipro and Infosys have done precisely that and overtaken some of the traditional business houses.

NEW MANAGEMENT STRATEGY

What should be the components of the new management strategy? These are principally four. First, the size of the company should be commercially viable. In the past, mainly because of the licensing restrictions, capacities had to be split and companies remained small although the size of the business group became large. The diversified business prevented specialisation and several companies could not acquire the economies of scale. It was precisely because of this the cost of production became generallv high and Indian companies, in spite of the low wages, were unable to withstand competition from imports. It will take time for these companies to grow to an economic size through the normal process of growth. The only way out is to amalgamate and merge. No wonder, in the past five years, the number of A&Ms has increased phenomenally. They have been more rampant in cement, banking, tyres, etc. in which size matters a great deal. There is considerable scope for consolidation and it will certainly take place in response to market compulsions.

Second, the Indian industry, partly because of the restrictions on royalty payments, did not go in for the state-of the-art technology. The result was that the quality of goods was not world class and the cost of production was prohibitive. Besides, labour laws came in the way of retrenchment that could have followed with the introduction of new technologies. The market is brutal and only those that are commercially efficient can ultimately win. So far, Indian industry did not even want to invest substantially in research and preferred to survive on borrowed technology. To be market leaders, it is important for corporates to be technology innovators. The challenge to Indian management is development of indigenous technologies, which can give it the edge in international competition.

NO MORE PROTECTION

Third, Indian industry was so far confined to the domestic market. Except for textiles, gems and jewellery and, to some extent, chemicals, it did not look for markets abroad. That was because, with the high cost and low quality of goods, it was not able to confront its competitors. With the globalisation that has already taken place and the further assimilation that will follow, Indian industry, if it adapts fast to the new situation, will be able to develop a market for its products. It should discuss with the Government measures that can improve its competitive ability rather than plead for protection. Industry, for instance, has been reluctant to accept a significant reduction in import tariffs. But, this itself can help promote exports because the cost of production will be lowered and this will open up opportunities to participate in the world market. Of course, that will not happen by itself. Enterprises will have to devise strategies to enter that market, possibly through active collaboration with trading companies abroad in the initial stages. Later on, after gaining experience, they can go it alone.

Our exports are not commensurate with the size of our economy. They are only about eight per cent of the GDP. China' s economy is only twice the size of our economy, but its exports are more than five times ours. The development of South East Asian economies has been brought about mainly by entry into the export market. It is important that our industry gets into this business not only to earn foreign exchange but also to prove to itself its own efficiency. In areas in which export is possible, companies should target exports at 25 per cent of their production.

Fourth, the management style will have to undergo a substantial change. Quite a few of the companies have already adopted measures of scientific management. There is considerable devolution of decision making by professional managers. And yet, the results are not the best that are possible. A mere replication of Western models of management will not work. Companies will have to discover their own management model, which is suitable for Indian conditions under Indian laws. Delegation of power has to be appropriately combined with accountability.

WIDENING DIMENSIONS

The dimensions of management have widened. It is no longer the domestic conditions that have to be considered but also conditions in the rest of the world. In their borrowing programme, for instance, companies will have to keep in mind the movement in exchange rates and protect themselves, through hedging against the relative interest rates in different markets, to be able to reduce the cost of funds. Corporate governance has also been a subject of considerable debate and will soon take legal form. Much more than the form, it is the content that matters. Managements should address themselves to maximisation of shareholder value, a dimension which has so far been very much neglected.

The new strategies are certainly finding a place in management. Many business houses have gained from the expertise provided by consultancy firms. However, the tempo of change is slow. Amalgamations have still to pick up pace. Market development has been initiated but is not yet aggressive. Management styles are beginning to change and have to be accelerated. As for investment in R&D, this is absolutely minimal. Perhaps, a collaborative effort between industry and organisations like CSIR can make a lot of difference. The overall aim should initially be to face up to competition from abroad and subsequently make inroads into the world market.

BUSINESS BEYOND BORDERS

—V. Raghuraman

Information Technology (IT) is revolutionalising our quality of life and is impacting ways of conducting business and is redefining literacy to the point where computer language is becoming the global *lingua franca.* The computer-communication nexus is churning out innovative knowledge services and products. In fact, knowledge service providers have emerged as the fastest growing segment of human activity in the early part of the new millennium. IT is creating a seamless world with business beyond borders being an inevitable fall-out.

ALL PERVASIVE

It is all pervasive and traverses all types of businesses. Internet's ease and hype have caught the fancy of Indian households and internet service providers are getting into the act of finding a niche to address this market. Further, large MNCs and Indian companies are offering user-friendly multimedia computers and printers for home use with added CD titles. Digital photography has immense potential and already we have several companies targeting homes with digital cameras and scanners. We have before us Web TV and Internet, with Videocon and BPL having already announced their

Mr. V. Raghuraman is Senior Advisor, Energy, CII. He earlier served as Secretary General, ASSOCHAM.

offering. Applications in education and R&D are in terms of real-time data acquisition equipment, high capacity storage devices and high-end workstations. The application software is generally being developed in-house, but pharmaceutical and related research organisations rely heavily on third-party applications in areas like molecular simulation. IT applications in business and industry are being targeted by maintenance vendors by way of routine customer support, facility management, network management, IT asset management, site planning, environmental engineering, structured cabling and so on. But, with maintenance and support growing in terms of opportunities as well as technical challenge, things might be changing for the better in the near future. The new order is of maintenance engineers being encouraged to get the requisite certification.

IT IS A MANAGEMENT FUNCTION

Two important parameters that control the performance of any service industry is the level of service and the corresponding cost incurred. Even small increases in service levels sometimes warrant disproportionate increases in the technology infrastructure. Unless IT-enabled service systems take on the job, it becomes very difficult to create customer lock-in. Use of IT in the airlines industry is moving beyond the area of passenger reservation and cargo to involve management functions. Aircraft maintenance engineering and crew scheduling are also becoming important areas. Traditionally, the airlines sector worldwide relies on outsourcing deals with technology service companies because the service uptime is very critical. IT applications in airport include automated gate readers, boarding card readers etc.

Use of IT in the publishing industry has gained maturity. Almost all the publishing majors like Bennett Coleman, The Indian Express Group and Living Media rely on IT for all internal and external publishing functions. Office automation beyond local area networking involving groupware and messaging is also spreading. The Times of India intranet implementation is a prime example of intranets in the country.

The hospitality sector too is gaining maturity in IT usage. The Taj Group, the Oberoi Group, the Welcome Group are some of the efficient users of IT in this industry. With most of back-office and front-office automation in place, the star-graded hotels are looking at harnessing IT for emerging applications like e-commerce and data warehousing to get to the next level of returns. The focus includes designing loyalty programmes and positioning on the internet to attract foreign business and tourists. Service is extremely cost-driven in the industry and efficient property management systems help in reigning control over costs. The Railways, however, have been lagging in terms of IT usage. After the big move towards computerised reservations, nothing new had been undertaken until some time back when the facility of online reservation was introduced. In this sense, the public sector undertaking is only looking at organic, not quantum, growth. Freight management, a big revenue earner for the Railways, still has only rudimentary IT components in its operations.

IT MANTRAS

Prompting companies to keep their plants rolling with better integration of business processes are mantras like ERP and CAD/CAM. The process-manufacturing sector traditionally spends more on IT because of the large number of companies engaged in this activity as well as their scale of operations. In general, the business and IT priorities of both process and discrete manufacturing are the same — controlling inventory, production and marketing costs, improving IT infrastructure, automating internal and external processes and better decision-making through use of IT on the information technology front. In the pharmaceuticals industry, the WTO agreement on patents has forced companies to get patents for their formulations. Clinical trials, a very data- intensive area, are fast emerging as an application in the pharma industry.

The major investment heads for a manufacturing company are: infrastructure, which includes systems, connectivity, messaging and design applications, databases application development and packaged application implementation services, consulting and other services and external connectivity connecting to dealers and suppliers. The emerging application is e-commerce. Many manufacturing organisations, especially in the private sector, have messaging and groupware in place for intra-organisational communication. Network-centric applications continue to be developed. ERP is the watchword in the manufacturing sector and the term has gained a substantial mindshare compared to marketshare in the past decade. With almost all global players present in the country, the stage is set for the launch of the Indian manufacturing sector into the age of integrated applications. The move towards ERP is a high investment proposition with accompanying investments in hardware, connectivity and implementation services, apart from a lot of invisible costs involved in process change, change management and training.

The process industry's focus is on integrating business applications with the plant floor. The major areas under consideration are finance, materials and sales and distribution. Since production in the process industry is plant-oriented, it falls within the realm of distributed digital control systems. The most important area after this is the maintenance function. Selection of a proper ERP package is based solely on business needs, essentially the fit that the product offers. CAD/CAM is the other major focus area for the manufacturing sector. Traditionally, the automotive and aerospace industries are the largest users of CAD/CAM. Increasing design capacity is also providing a competitive edge. There is a trend towards reverse engineering, especially in the engineering and appliances industry. Product data management is a further leading edge of CAD/CAM philosophy. For the supplier, it means enhanced competence, apart from improved competitiveness. Many suppliers with their improved design capacity and integration in GEMs have also started exporting. Another reason for the importance of design is the improved alignment that many manufacturing organisations have acquired through business process re-engineering.

THRUSTS IN BANKING

The investments made by the banking sector can be broadly characterised by a continuation of IT automation plans by large public sector banks, implementation of connectivity and leading-edge technology solutions by the newer private sector banks, continuing branch automation and branch connectivity by the older private banks and refinements in service by the cooperative banking sector. There has been a heavy outlay in renovation of offices, rendering of value added services schemes and a shift to card culture through cash dispensers and ATMs. The broad direction of IT usage points towards a continuation of refinements in key application areas like loan appraisal systems, policy management, decision-support systems and funds management. Technologies like groupware are now being used by almost everyone because of the collaborative nature of work in FIs and credit rating agencies.

While insurance companies like LIC, GIC and Oriental Insurance had invested in connectivity and policy management, UTI's thrust was on production systems. NSE's priorities were disaster recovery systems, datawarehousing, market surveillance and settlement systems. From an applications point of view, apart from operational automation areas like general ledger, inter-branch reconciliation, and bank-wide MIS, the main IT-centric applications that have gained maturity are cash management and treasury management. These crucial banking functions are now actively addressed using the latest technology. Retail banking using network applications like electronic funds transfer (EFT) and those relevant to branch banking have caught the attention of many public and private sector banks. To facilitate these applications, a share payment network system, Swadhan, had been set up in 1998. Swadhan is a large network of ATMs spread over Mumbai and connected to a central hub. The services offered under the network include cash withdrawal, balance inquiry, cash/cheque deposit, funds transfer, requests for cheque book, standing instructions and accounts statement. The other network that has come up is the IDRBT (Institute of Development and Research in Banking

Technology) network. Its central hub located in Hyderabad handles data switching, network monitoring and supporting multiple user groups. As a VSAT network, it supports TDM/TDMA and hybrid network structures. The applications of the IDRBT network would be: data traffic between banks and FIs, isolated traffic in virtual bank groups, fax traffic between banks and FIs, isolated traffic in virtual bank groups, fax traffic, voice traffic between banks in mesh network and video-conferencing at select sites. Messaging involves enhancing customer collaboration using knowledge sharing, information dissemination and better service delivery channels. The key benefit sought is to strengthen customer relationships.

OIL AND POWER SECTORS

In the oil and power sectors, the thrust has been on large-scale infrastructure upgradation and systems integration projects, which are addressed by large vendors of national repute, capable of providing implementation and support services in a large number of remote locations. The common line running through them is the nature of process generation, transmission and distribution. The latest pre-occupation with IT has been more customer responsive and competitive. What happens in oil refineries is optimisation of processes to ensure maximum safety as well as output, minimum wastage and upgradation in the future with the eventual linking of geographically balanced distribution processes. In short, maximising on production efficiency is the target towards which oil refineries work. IT plays an important role here in helping them achieve this target as easily and as productively as possible. Today, distributed digital control (DDCS) is common place with refineries taking to this device of automation in a major way. For this purpose, the major refineries are now either installing or upgrading DDCS and also integrating the outputs of refinery MIS to those of the central corporate MIS of the company. One very significant area is the artificial intelligence system, where it enables a business model- based prediction for refinery processes that are addressed by DDCS. This will have a higher level of computer control whereby all the refinery processes could be designed for the future.

DEMANDS OF TELECOM

Business imperatives do drive IT acquisition in the telecom sector also, though not from a competitive standpoint. Applications of IT are focused on customer acquisition and retention, market segmentation and prospect identification, targeted campaign, promotion, customer schemes, tariff plans, total customer management facility, churn prediction and prevention, analysis of connections, disconnections and reconnections, dealer analysis and monitoring, revenue enhancement, profitability analysis, analysis of accounts receivable, product sales analysis, bill assurance, economic modeling, network utilisation and capacity planning. In an industry like telecom, winners will be those who can adapt quickly to new market opportunities. Against this backdrop, telecom providers need mission-critical information technology solutions that can continue performance and scalability along with flexibility and modularity.

END IN SIGHT

Jack Welch once said, "when the rate of change inside the corporation is slower than outside, the end is in sight" — an apt statement in this era of new business paradigm. Sparked off by the PC revolution of the eighties and nineties, computing power has been brought into the hands of millions of users. The internet is like the giant and the intricated web is providing connectivity faster and faster. Internet is rapidly gaining popularity, both worldwide as well as in India. This can be seen from the fact that personal computers took about 16 years to reach 50 million people whereas connectivity alone, i.e. internet, has reached the same number of people in four years' time. However, currently, internet is now mainly used as a medium of rapid information gathering and dissemination. With enhancements in network bandwidths, security methods and electronic fund transfer techniques, internet is now being viewed as a platform for carrying out business. E-commerce and e-business have been the buzzwords of recent years. People would like to shop from the comfort of their homes, pay by credit cards and receive home delivery. Companies would like to reach hitherto untapped markets, cut out the middleman (distributor, dealer, retailer etc.) and get to the customer directly, thereby decreasing transaction costs. This has led to a massive interest in internet as a platform for e-commerce, which in turn represents another paradigm of a business transaction.

E-COMMERCE

Business applications now need to work with e-commerce solutions. When someone places an order for, say a book, the application needs to immediately tell the person the inventory status and the number of days it would take to despatch the book. This is a classic example of B2C (Business to Consumer) type of e-commerce interaction. Another major area in e-commerce is B2B (Business to Business). This has been at a nascent stage in the United States itself and is taking roots in India. Here, companies register into a B2B website or a e-commerce "portal" as it is called, as buyers or sellers. Buyers put out their request for quotations including tender documents on the portal, along with drawings and other specifications. Sellers designing to submit bids can peruse the documents and can submit their bids online. The evaluation process can be made as transparent as desired by the buyer. The award of contract and subsequent documentation, like purchase order, delivery notes and invoices can also be carried out over the internet.

B2B introduces another level of requirement, which presently needs to transcend boundaries between different brands and interact with applications of other brands used by other portal members. All this needs to happen over the internet. Seamless integration with payment modes like credit card, cybercash and cybercheque is required. For India to be a part of this fraternity, we needed to have cyber-laws and these were duly put in place. Vendors have worked at a feverish pace to prepare their products for B2C as well as B2B applications. Graphonet and similar companies have taken up sub-portals within large portals (General Electric's Trading Partner Network or TPN was an obvious example) to facilitate e-commerce through their packages. In the United States, internet-effected transactions of goods and services were of the order of $ 300 billion in 2002 against on-line transactions worth $42 billion in 1997. It is estimated that the net transactions double every 100 days.

CYBER SHOPPING

According to Forester Research, B2B e-commerce had accounted for 78 per cent of the total cyber transactions in 2000. By end of 2002,

- 43% of durable goods with sales close to $100 billion
- wholesale office supplies, electronic goods and scientific equipment worth $89 billion.
- doctors and lawyers $ 19 billion
- travel industry $74 billion
- computer hardware and software $ 3.8 billion
- books, music, entertainment $ 3.8 billion were effected through cyber-shopping, in the assessment of Forester Research.

Cyber shopping has no opening or closing hours. It has global connectivity and web standards, available for transactions 24 hours a day, seven days a week. Virtual shops can be created where product/service information can be sourced and details of comparable products perused, prices and services analysed, customer reaction ascertained, and transaction enacted. Thus, a sea change will be seen with an improved service level — with hitherto unknown and uninitiated clients being introduced — thereby enhancing customer access, lending speed to market, reducing cycle time, introducing new products and services with least time delays, improving brand recognition and reducing distribution costs.

THE FLIPSIDE

Of course, every good product or service has its flipside. E-commerce is not an exception. Investments are needed to ensure security. Security is the likely bugbear for e-commerce transactions. Like pockets getting picked, credit cards misused involve security risks. E-commerce would need in-built confidence and provide assurance to transactors to make them feel good with cyber-shopping. It is going to take a long while for us to get there. Gnan.com had taken the lead to be ahead of the pack. Thus, there is a surge, upsetting traditional ways of conducting business. The e-business wave is comparable with historic events like the industrial revolution. Those who took advantage, be it companies or countries, rose to power and glory. We are yet again at the crossroads of history and are witnessing the birth of a new revolution, that of e-business. It has the power to soar us to new heights.

A number of start-ups have been witnessed in India as well. Gnan.com aspired to be the leading Indian network of shopping on and off. It sought to inspire a spirit of belonging among sections of the community in pursuit of not just information but knowledge that touched our everyday life. It epitomised the goal to position itself as a pioneer in cyber shopping. Initial cyber-shopping services targetted the prime customers but moved towards others later on. Information technology in the worldwide scenario has evolved greatly in the past decade and affects day-to-day life. IT usage in India has also gained considerable ground and now state-of-the art products and solutions are available almost concurrently with their global release. The role of IT is only going to increase in the new millenium. Thus, business beyond borders is a massive reality with IT as the driving force.

12

A PARTICIPATORY APPROACH —HUDCO's MANAGEMENT STYLE

—V. Suresh

In order to be successful, organisations have to create for themselves a strong, resilient, innovative and collaborative environment so as to promote wide trust and a sense of professional association rather than a narrow employer-employee ethos. A sense of common purpose and a goal of collective excellence would enable institutions succeed better than professional excellence or managerial capabilities alone. In this respect, HUDCO's approach to management is worth highlighting. HUDCO is the premier techno-financing institution in the field of housing and urban development in India. Established in 1970, the company has contributed towards provision of homes for over nine million families and implementation of 757 urban infrastructure schemes — comprising utility infrastructure spread over water supply, sewerage, drainage, solid waste management and transport projects, social infrastructure schemes covering health, education and recreational facilities and economic and commercial infrastructure involving office and shopping complexes.

Mr. V. Suresh is Chairman & Managing Director, HUDCO.

HUMAN RESOURCE BASE

Started in Delhi in 1970, HUDCO has today five zonal offices for the north, east, north-east, west and south and has 28 regional/development offices to cover operations in all the states and union territories. With over 1,000 employees, of both the executive and non- executive cadre, the Corporation is predominantly a professional institution of multifarious disciplines. A strong human resource base has proved to be among the best assets of HUDCO to play its positive role in the housing and urban development sector. The PSU's management style primarily is based on a participatory approach.

We have decentralised our activities to a great extent by giving considerable autonomy to the executive directors. Autonomy also brings with it greater responsibility and creates a result-oriented environment. Our operations are built on a strong social commitment. We are project-oriented and we seek to ensure that projects are affordable to the target groups and are at the same time technically sound. Every year, 55 per cent of the housing portfolio resources are allocated for schemes addressing the requirements of economically weaker sections and low-income households. Our motto says it better — profitability with social justice. HUDCO also supports various NGOs. An extensive on-the-job experience provided through participation in conferences and training programmes is one of the hallmarks of HUDCO's strategy to keep its personnel abreast of developments in various fields of specialisation. HUDCO itself organises and supports a number of conferences and seminars pertaining to the housing and urban development sector. The emphasis is on learning and on the latest innovations and initiatives. Our thrust is on empowering officers and staff of HUDCO as well as those of our borrowing agencies. We are very clear about not having a strong HUDCO with weak borrowing agencies.

TEAM PLAYERS

We must empower people, as then they will manage with passion. We need team players and not individual performers because none of us individually is smarter than all of us together. Today, employee retention has become a major concern with most organisations and in retaining them we build an open culture, which recognises talent and performance and prepares staff for change proactively. HUDCO strives to provide careers to its employees and not just jobs. The challenge today is not only of learning but also unlearning a lot of things, which may act as hurdles in the learning process. We have our own Human Settlement Management Institute (HSMI), which caters to the needs of capacity building, not only of HUDCO's employees but also of those involved in the housing and urban development sector. HSMI has been imparting training since 1991 and organising workshops and policy seminars on specialised areas of housing and infrastructure development and has imparted training to nearly 10,000 professionals from various housing boards, development authorities, infrastructure development agencies, local bodies, professional institutions and NGOs / CBOs. HSMI has also developed a decentralised training network for imparting training to grassroots level professionals and workers in Karnataka, Maharashtra, Rajasthan, Uttar Pradesh, Orissa and West Bengal, the North Eastern Region and Kerala with appropriate linkages with state level training agencies covering the human settlement sector.

TOMORROW IS TODAY

We are fully aware of the present predicament of business operations. Tomorrow is today for managers. As Jack Welch says, "if you think you are going to be successful in running your business the next 10 years the way you did in the last 10 years, you are out of your mind. To succeed, you have to disturb the present."Merely catching up is not enough to face up to the managerial challenges. Organisations have to equip managers with push growth strategies to elevate the spirit, reorganise the talent and implement the strategies in their proper form. Even to maintain your present "standing" one has to keep running, as others are running faster to catch up. In my view, the new millennium would be one of specialisation in all respects and, at the same time, it would be one in which everyone would require to be informed of almost everything. Division of labour would guide the rapidity of growth. Information would be power and the ability of individuals to succeed would primarily depend on the earnestness of individuals to remain informed and gain access to information. The winner would have to be pro-active in his approach to identifying the opportunities, assessing the risks and addressing the issues to achieve the goals. The end goal needs to remain the first priority.

FROM BUSY-NESS TO BUSINESS

As the CEO of a premier techno-financing institution, I feel that there are a few imperatives, which we need to adhere to, to achieve success in our endeavours. Time has become crucial since we all are short of time, but we must analyse whether we really are busy doing the things that deserve the time spent. In this age of information technology and innovations in simplification of processes, and cutting through red-tape, if we are still busy doing nothing really worthwhile then we need to assess the reasons. We must move from the so-called busy-ness to business. Once the process of business thinking comes into enterprises, it would be much easier to manage as we will be able to relate ourselves and our functions to value addition. Future benefits will accrue from human intellect more than from any other resource like land, natural resources or capital. Even HRD's role would be strategic in facilitating organisations to prepare for the morrow. Chanakya, the great strategist, also supported this strategic vision in management thousands of years ago. A quick responsiveness, a pro-active approach to developmental issues and an added sense of responsibility are needed to guide the operational behaviour of institutions and have to be imbedded in the organisational culture.

Constant changes and updating are the pre-requisites of sustained success in the new millennium. Reform is not a one-time process. We need to be prevented from change on a continuing basis. We need to be one not just to accept change but to expect change. The Nobel Laureate, Dr. Amartya Sen has said, "the need now is to correct Governmental under-activity in social areas". In today's environment, if companies contribute to the society, they don't do any favour by that, because community is not only a part of our business in the larger context but they are also emerging as stakeholders in our organisations. Corporates have a major role to play in this segment as they can provide the support and infrastructure to the social issues, which in turn give them not only a human face but also wider acceptability.

13

NOT AN EASY TASK FOR MANAGERS

—Y.K. Gupta

Stronger than all the armies of the world is an idea whose time has come, wrote Victor Hugo, the French writer. Internet globalisation is one such invincible idea. It is the backbone of the global economic system in the 21st century. Technological changes and accelerated globalisation have brought in their wake many expectations and concerns. But, there is no doubt that the future is bright and rich with opportunities, which even the most incorrigible of optimists cannot have envisaged. The task of the manager today is not easy. This functionary is at the centre of a rapidly evolving world. Issues, problems and markets are different and much more complex. Today is different from yesterday and tomorrow will be still more different and tougher than today. Quality, cost and delivery driven-markets will decide the role and task of the manager. Being a successful manager requires an integrated approach to developing new skills.

LEARNING IN BUSINESS

This makes learning a critical factor in business, and knowledge an essential requisite. Without knowledge there cannot be any creativity. Greater the knowledge the more the

---

Mr. Y.K. Gupta has served as General Manager, Larsen & Toubro.

patterns, combinations and ideas that are possible. A manager, thus, must give a serious thought to self-development, self-empowerment and to re-tooling himself to build his core strengths and capabilities, expand his personal intelligence and strengthen will power. In an intangible world, one needs a clear vision, a focused strategy and a sense of purpose apart from values, new perspectives and a soul capable of transforming the cultural initiative.

This work-out must be seen as a continuous effort to achieve boundary-less management behaviour on the one hand and endless pursuit of the best idea on the other. The key is to learn and to add more value today and day after day. With knowledge one reinvents himself by organising his beliefs as well as values. Organisations are a reflection of their managers and an organisational transformation brings with it the personal transformation of the manager.

The transformational leadership or self-leadership, thus developed, expands the latter's sense of reality, in the process refining his perspective, thinking and his level of inner wisdom, compassion, sensitivity, empathy, analysis, adaptiveness, challenge and, finally, control. The manager can, therefore, analyse what is winning today to determine its future vulnerability.

UNFORESEEN DEMANDS

The age of internet globalisation has imposed unforeseen demands on individuals, organisations and nations. Multinationals with their fast changing technologies have brought in a new work culture. This is forcing itself on investors, lenders, shareholders, FIIs and NGOs. Government policies, public perceptions and values of organisational growth are also changing as a consequence. Thus, the manager of the morrow has to work with diversity. It will be impossible for him to be competent if he cannot value and manage diversity. An intense understanding of the market becomes essential in this context. Gaining added knowledge is an important tool and harnessing potential knowledge requires a wide exposure besides immense experience. But, knowledge alone does not guarantee the formation of new patterns. An integrated diversity perception multiplies managerial value. Experience leads to a quick and appropriate response and a capacity for creative planning, as well as daring and a risk-taking attitude. Data get accumulated in a person from his or her total life experience. These data are played upon constantly by current inputs through the senses. Experience makes a manager a flexible or a multi-track thinker, who deliberates on experience with a multitude of approaches, so as to adapt quickly to a changed environment, and finds appropriate solutions for emerging problems.

We can learn from each other both knowledge and experience. Collective learning will lead to quick and appropriate responses. This collaborative approach will maximise returns and a cap on uneconomical use of resources. We would be able to expand business without putting too much pressure on shareholders and to sustain a competitive advantage in what can be described as non-forgiving markets. Success truly is the result of good judgement based on knowledge. Good judgement, in turn, is the result of shared experience. In order to succeed, one must have a long-term focus. Success and failure are not overnight experiences. Success is the result of deciding to hold oneself to a higher and an ever rising standard and deciding to feed one's mind rather than allowing the environment to control him. A number of small decisions taken by a multiplicity of managers independently and at different times help create knowledge and experience, leading to great success at times.

CONCLUSION

There has never been anything like an essentially academic effort, not certainly in economics and related disciplines. Keynes might not have visualised the kind of response to his *General Theory* when he wrote it, but he had addressed his *Magnum Opus* not to the academia but to policy makers and the market place. He had no doubt about his audience. That the U.S. President of the time, Mr. Franklin Roosevelt, grappling with the aftermath of the Great Depression, found in Keynesianism a recipe for the recovery of the U.S. economy was only to be expected.

This study certainly is no *General Theory*, but considering that the existing literature on management is not always focussed sharply on the market place, the effort has a thrust that should not be dismissed lightly. The experts involved have dealt with matters that compel attention. Serving managers as well as the young men and women preparing for a future in management, surely, would find in their offering a lot to ponder over.

The two parts taken together have a strong topical thrust and should help generate a healthy public debate. One can only hope that the missing link in India Inc. will be found sooner rather than later and diverse players are finally ready for the battle instead of moaning as they have been doing all this long that the rivals are much too strong for them.

INDEX

❑❑❑